THE GLUTEN-FREE GUT HEALTH PLAN & COOKBOOK FOR BEGINNERS

60 DAY LEAKY GUT SOLUTION TO RESTORE YOUR HEALTH BY ELIMINATING CHRONIC PAIN, INFLAMMATION, AND STUBBORN WEIGHT GAIN

7 DAY MEAL PLAN W/21 DELICIOUS & SIMPLE GF AND VEGAN RECIPES.

Written By
PURETURE, HHP

CONTENTS

Introduction — 5

1. What's So Bad About Gluten? — 11
2. The Effect of Gluten on Your Body and Mind — 35
3. Gluten and the Gut: Are They Mortal Enemies? — 66
4. How Gluten Hides in Popular Foods and Products — 79
5. The Gluten-Free Diet - a Road to Health — 104
6. Creating A Gluten-Free Habit — 127
7. 7 Day Gluten-Free & Plant-Based Meal Plan with 21 Recipes — 154

Conclusion — 193
References — 199

© Copyright 2020 - All rights reserved.

It is not legal to reproduce, duplicate, or transmit any part of this document in either electronic means or in printed format. Recording of this publication is strictly prohibited and any storage of this document is not allowed unless with written permission from the publisher except for the use of brief quotations in a book review.

INTRODUCTION

"Yet an estimated 99 percent of people who have a problem with eating gluten don't even know it. They ascribe their ill health to symptoms to something else - not gluten sensitivity, which is 100 percent curable."

— MARK HYMAN, M.D.

There are all types of statistics telling us how many people suffer with gluten intolerance in just the United States alone. The number is in the millions, anywhere between 3 and 6 million depending on who is doing the research and reporting. What gets me every time is the quote above. While millions are living with known gluten sensitivity, there are tens, perhaps hundreds, of millions who have problems with gluten and don't even know it.

"An estimated 99 percent" of us. Let that sink in for a minute. Think of all the chronic health issues we as a society are suffering from today. How so many people feel powerless against their ill health and turn to medications as a saving grace, except pharmaceuticals often treat the symptoms but rarely the root cause

In this case, we're looking at gluten as the root cause of many of the ailments that plague us today. The relationship we have with gluten is complicated. Gluten itself is harmless. It's nothing more than a group of proteins that are found primarily in grains. For generations upon generations, we've managed to coexist with gluten. So, why has it become such a hot topic in the health industry? Why are so many more of us seeing and feeling the negative effects of gluten, and why is the incidence of Celiac disease skyrocketing compared to years past?

These are all questions we need answered but all you know right now is that you're tired of not feeling right. Maybe you've recently been diagnosed with Celiac disease after a long road of painful symptoms, endless doctor visits, and more than your fair share of worry. If you have Celiac disease, you've witnessed first-hand how severe the effects of gluten are in certain people.

Perhaps you're someone who either suspects gluten sensitivity, or have done enough research on your own to know you just have too much gluten in your life, and you want to bring things back into a healthy balance. If so, you're in the company of millions. No matter what your surface reason for being here, it all comes down to your health, and your desire to improve it.

What we're learning about gluten is that it doesn't "just" cause digestive discomfort. Science is beginning to connect the dots and the picture is telling us that too much gluten can lead to gastrointestinal conditions but also headaches, chronic fatigue, skin condition, neurological disorders, depression, anxiety...the list goes on. I probably don't even have to tell you this because you're already feeling it.

The challenging aspect of controlling the effects of gluten is that each person is affected in different ways. There isn't a one size fits all approach here. There is no point in preaching that you should shun all gluten because it worked for me. You could be someone who is mildly affected, or maybe you don't feel any symptoms, but you want to get control before they begin to manifest. My journey doesn't apply to you because I want you to heal in the way YOU need.

That said, I've felt compelled to write this book for some time now. My personal experience with gluten has been transformative. I felt the shift in my own body. I researched endlessly to learn more about the effects of gluten and why we're suffering from them so much right now. I've guided clients through their gluten-free paths and watched them take back control of their health. As the good doctor says in the quote above, gluten-sensitivity is 100 percent curable. It requires no special pill, zero invasive and expensive tests, and your schedule doesn't need to be packed with doctor's appointments. All you need is the willingness to do it and stick with it.

My goal with this book has been to provide you with real information about gluten and gluten-sensitivity. It's good to know what gluten does to sensitive individuals but it's equally important to know how and why this happens. When you have this type of knowledge, you're no longer going off on a whim based on what someone else says. You have the power to make educated decisions about your health and the choices you make.

This book is designed as a 60-day plan to move you from feeling sick and tired to embracing the freedom that optimal health brings. We talk about this later in the book, but it takes about 60 days for a habit to form. If you can stick with this for just 60 days, you can kick the gluten-habit and improve your health in so many ways.

What you're not going to find here is someone holding your hand and telling you what to do. With this book, I'm here to help guide you through my own experience, both personally and with my clients. I've done the legwork of research and provided you with everything you need. What I need you to do is determine what you want from a health standpoint. Only you know how severely gluten affects you, and to what degree you want to eliminate it from your life. Each journey is different. That is why I've presented this book as a toolbox and suggestions on how to build something great. This isn't a micromanaged diet plan but instead one you help create yourself so that you're more likely to be successful at it.

Recommendation from the Pureture Wellness team:

We would like to make this journey you are about to embark on as smooth as possible. As with any journey, preparations need to be made, and there are tools fit for each pilgrimage. In our case we require the Detox Goodies Toolkit, which is completely free. Not using these tools is like making a trip to a rainforest and not taking any sort of tool to protect yourself from mosquitoes. You can do it, but the experience won't be quite as seamless as it could have been. It is discomfort that is not necessary and can even be risky. This analogy fits perfectly; if you don't have the right tools to go through with this process it can be uncomfortable, and there is even a risk of failure involved.

Please access the following link: https://www.pureture.com/detox-goodies/

In this link you will find the following components:

- 20 Daily Detox Tips
- 15 Detox Tea Formulas
- 10 Detox Juices
- Master Shopping List: Healing & Detox Food

It may not be completely clear why these components are essential quite yet, but in further chapters you will notice that this information will be very helpful. When you actually begin the practical side of the work, you will come to understand. These tools are meant to alleviate some stress and obstacles that may show up along the way.

Are you ready to heal your gut, reclaim your health, and refuse to fall victim to chronic disease that's influenced by dietary choices? Great, let's get started.

1

WHAT'S SO BAD ABOUT GLUTEN?

The gluten-free diet is at the very top of a list of today's hottest diet trends, right up there with Paleo and Keto. Once a way of eating enters "trend diet" status, you can guarantee that there's going to be a lot of talking from people on both sides of the table. What we need to realize is that gluten-free is more than a passing trend. For millions of people with Celiac disease, non-Celiac gluten sensitivity, and other conditions that make them sensitive to gluten, eliminating or reducing gluten is necessary for their health.

In my opinion, one of the most frustrating aspects of the gluten-free "trend" is the overwhelming amount of misinformation that the average person encounters. It takes no time at all to do a quick Google search and land on a gluten-free blog written by someone who speaks with authority, although they're going off of no more than personal experience and unproven theories.

I want to say that these types of blogs aren't all bad. The people who run them are helping to build a community of support for those who are living a gluten-free life. My issue is that, despite their best intentions, they also contribute to the misinformation that's being spread around. Those opposed to being gluten-free aren't much better, often referencing incomplete data to make a point that could eventually harm the health of the person reading it.

I want to start this book by clearing up as many of these misconceptions as possible. I'm coming at this as someone who has helped people with gluten intolerance and sensitivity rebuild their health by eliminating gluten, and I've experienced the positive benefits of a gluten-free diet in my own life. You could say that I'm biased but I'm also focused on helping you improve your health. Gluten-free isn't ideal for everyone, and I openly admit that.

However, I do feel that reducing or eliminating gluten can have positive effects for many of you reading this, and not just those of you who are living with Celiac disease or non-Celiac gluten sensitivity. My goal in this chapter is to provide you with a solid foundation of information about gluten and gluten-related health conditions, so that you can eventually make your own informed decisions about the role of gluten in your life and whether you're ready to take the next steps forward to reducing or eliminating it from your diet.

One of the first, and most important, areas of misconception I've noticed is where gluten comes from. Gluten is found in grains, including:

- Wheat
- Rye
- Barley
- Triticale
- Brewer's yeast
- Malt
- Wheat starch
- Derivatives of wheat, including wheat berries, durum, spelt, semolina, Farro, and Kamut, along with a few lesser-known wheat derivatives.

These are the basics, but we'll dig a little deeper to help you identify those sneakier sources a little later in the book.

So, are you ready to get started? Great because I'm excited to begin this learning and healing journey with you!

DEMYSTIFYING GLUTEN

Over the past decade or so, gluten has become a major buzzword in the diet and health industry. The term "gluten-free" can be found on countless products that line the aisles of practically every grocery store, and I've lost track of how many books and blogs exist on the subject.

In other words, it has been practically impossible to avoid the gluten-free mega-trend the past several years. With the phrase being everywhere, it's surprising how much is misunderstood about gluten, what it is, and what it does.

I want to start by defining gluten as simply as possible. Gluten, this thing you want to avoid, is nothing more than a name for a family of proteins. Protein is another hot buzzword in the diet and health industries, but gluten is different from the protein you find in foods like animal meats, beans, and some vegetables.

Gluten is a word used to describe a category of proteins found in some grains. If you want to visualize gluten, imagine digging your fingers into a bowl of fresh bread dough. That stickiness, the way it resists a little when you attempt to pull it apart...that is gluten in action. It creates this sort of sticky matrix that produces the texture that makes bread and baked goods so irresistible to so many people.

But gluten doesn't just magically appear when you mix flour and water. If that were the case, you could simply avoid the bread aisle and be good. Gluten is found in the grain itself, which makes it exponentially more difficult to avoid, especially considering the number of processed foods that include some sort of ingredient that contains gluten.

Gluten works as a binder, and it's also heat-stable, which makes it perfect (at least in the eyes of processed food manufacturers) for providing texture and maintaining moisture in processed foods. Gluten has been snuck into many of the convenience foods we eat today. Eliminating gluten from one's diet involves learning to recognize stealthily labeled ingredients and accepting that so many of the foods marketed for their "taste and convenience" are a no-go on a gluten-free diet.

I mentioned that gluten is a family of proteins found in grains. We tend to think of gluten as a singular compound when it's an umbrella term for many different proteins, each capable of affecting your health in different ways. The two main gluten proteins are called glutenin and gliadin.

As if the fact that there are different types of gluten proteins isn't enough, gluten, as a compound, is extremely complex. When looking at wheat alone, each type of wheat with a different genetic composition, or even wheat that is grown under different conditions, also possess unique gluten qualities. This is why some people might find that they experience random bouts of gluten intolerance, or that they're more sensitive to gluten that comes from one type of grain but not others.

Glutenin Vs. Gliadin

Between the two main gluten compounds - glutenin and gliadin - it's gliadin that has proven itself to be the real trouble maker for people with gluten sensitivity or intolerance. There are both similarities and differences between glutenin and gliadin, but the main difference is that gliadin contains epitopes, which are specific peptide sequences. In the simplest terms, these epitopes are resistant to the body's digestive processes. Long story short, gliadins form structures that are capable of bringing about an immune reaction and stimulate a T cell response.

Gliadin can initiate an immune response, even in the absence of a true pathogenic threat. When this happens, inflammation occurs, and normal gut function is disrupted. Given time, this inflammation will subside, and the gut will begin to heal itself - our bodies are remarkable that way.

However, in the case of gluten, or more specifically, gliadin, one might not be aware that the foods they're consuming are creating this inflammatory response. Because the body is so efficient at its job, internal inflammation isn't always immediately noticeable. So, we continue to consume gluten, completely unaware of the inflammatory processes going on, until we begin to notice some initial symptoms - bloating, gas, and general digestive upset. This process is the seed that grows into full-blown gluten sensitivity and intolerance.

For some, especially those with Celiac disease, gluten intolerance isn't so subtle as it introduces itself. Some people with Celiac disease experience a sudden onset of painful and concerning symptoms. It's important to realize that gluten can affect people in different ways, and with different severity. One person's gluten sensitivity is going to look completely different from another person's experience with Celiac's disease.

The Gluten-Free Craze: Trend, Hype, or Truth?

Over the past decade, perhaps arguably longer, there has been an incredible push toward living a gluten-free lifestyle. Some swear by living gluten-free, even though they have never officially been diagnosed with Celiac disease or even any degree of gluten intolerance. Then others claim gluten-free is truly beneficial for a small fraction of people, and that the rest of us are damaging our health rather than protecting it by eliminating gluten from our diets.

So, what's the scoop? Is eliminating gluten something that is generally beneficial from a health standpoint, or have we all just jumped on this trend blindly? In all honesty, and I'll explain my thoughts in greater detail, the answer is both.

Gluten is found in whole grains like wheat, rye, and barley - foods that we generally think of as being healthy, and they are. Grains are high in fiber, which the standard American diet is abysmally low in. They're also rich in B vitamins, minerals, and are good sources of protein for people following a plant-based diet. Considering this, it seems negligent to say these types of whole grains are straight-up bad for everybody. When everybody started jumping on the "gluten is bad" train, what the diet industry failed to address was that when the average person without a true gluten sensitivity eliminates these main sources of gluten, they're also eliminating foods that have major health benefits.

Let me first say, that when I speak of gluten-containing foods, I'm referring to healthy whole-grains - not processed foods that are void of any real nutritional value. Also, when I say that gluten-containing foods do offer nutritional and health benefits, I'm not saying this about people who struggle, sometimes quite painfully, with their relationship to gluten. What I am addressing is the gluten-free trend that so many jumped on without fully understanding the risks, along with the benefits.

I fully believe it's important to weigh both sides of the gluten issue evenly, and not present gluten in a completely negative light. Some people honestly have no issue tolerating gluten, and for them, the risks of a gluten-free diet can outweigh the benefits.

If you've been following a gluten-free diet, or are considering it as a way to bring about positive changes in your health, it's important that you pay close attention to balancing what your diet will lack by going gluten-free. This means ensuring that your diet contains ample fiber (25-30 grams per day), mostly from plant sources. It means making sure that you're consuming rich sources of B vitamins, or taking a good supplement, and it means replacing that part of your diet with nutrient-dense foods, and not processed gluten-free alternatives or foods that are high in sugars or saturated fats.

We also have multiple studies that have looked at the benefits of gluten in the diet. In my opinion, the benefits aren't of gluten specifically but rather of the inclusion of whole grains that happen to contain gluten. For example, there appears to be a link between cultures that consume lots of whole grains and overall better health outcomes for their population. There is also research that points to the possibility of an increased risk of cardiovascular disease for non-celiac individuals who follow a gluten-free diet. Again, it's the fiber and nutrient-dense grain consumption that is behind these results.

Is it possible to live a healthy life while being gluten-free? Absolutely, but it's also important to note that for people with no indications of gluten sensitivity, there may be more benefits to keeping gluten in their diet and eliminating other types of non-healthy foods.

WHEN GLUTEN BECOMES A PROBLEM

Celiac disease is one of the most widely known and severe forms of gluten-intolerance. While the exact number of people living with Celiac disease is unknown, it's estimated that the condition affects about 1% of the population in the United States. That equals out to about 3 million people, which is a huge number. However, in the grand scheme of things, Celiac disease is relatively rare, affecting about only 1 out of every 100 people.

A decade ago, Celiac disease was relatively unheard of, where today, many people instantly associate the condition with gluten intolerance. Our awareness of gluten and its potential negative effects on health has grown exponentially. Again, exact numbers are difficult to come by because dietary trends and preferences are fluid, but it's estimated that the number of people going gluten-free has tripled over the past decade. Some of these conversions are represented by a growing number of both diagnosed and undiagnosed Celiac disease. However, a significant number, a majority actually, comes from people who are avoiding gluten without a Celiac diagnosis.

A Gallup poll from a few years ago showed that about 1 in 5 Americans are consciously choosing to include gluten-free foods in their diets. The overwhelming majority of these individuals have not been diagnosed with, or are suspected to have Celiac disease, so what is it that's sparking such a noticeable preference toward gluten-free foods?

We can blame part of this on hype from the diet industry but to put all the blame on that would not only be shortsighted, it would also allude to the idea that people are nothing more than puppets that bow to suggestion when it comes to their health. In my experience, both personal and with my clients, I have found that this isn't the case.

Personally, I know that when I transitioned into reducing the amount of gluten-containing foods in my diet, I did so based on knowledge, research, and an acknowledgment of what I was experiencing with my own body. I am not someone who has been diagnosed with Celiac disease, but I have most definitely improved my health by eliminating damaging foods, gluten being one of them, that triggered unhealthy responses in my body. Each of us tolerates gluten differently. Some simply can't tolerate it at all, some have no issues, and then many others like me fall somewhere along the middle of the spectrum.

What I am noticing is that there seem to be more people who are experiencing changes in their health, doing their own research, having discussions with their medical care providers, and wondering if gluten is the culprit. I'm also seeing people who are living with a range of chronic health problems and wondering if eliminating gluten could be beneficial in relieving their symptoms.

An interesting example of chronic health conditions that may be affected by gluten intake is autoimmune disease. An autoimmune disease is a chronic condition in which the body's immune system mistakes healthy tissues for invasive pathogens and generates an immune response. Celiac disease falls under the umbrella of autoimmune disease.

We know that when a person is diagnosed with any one of a large number of autoimmune disorders, they are more likely to develop a second autoimmune condition. It's estimated that 25% of people with autoimmune disease will develop a separate autoimmune condition in their lifetime. Of course, this number fluctuates based on factors such as the age of onset and the type of initial autoimmune disorder.

The issue with gluten, outside of its role in Celiac disease, is that for many people it's an inflammatory trigger. This becomes more of a problem in people with autoimmune disease because every autoimmune condition involves increased levels of chronic inflammation that are present due to the immune system being continually switched on. Introduce an inflammation trigger like gluten, and it can make the symptoms of autoimmune conditions more severe.

This is why more people with autoimmune disease, and the people who care about them, are expressing great interest in the potential of a gluten-free diet in relieving the severity of symptoms.

Still, I think it's a safe point to say that the majority of people who are following the gluten-free trend are doing so not based on a diagnosis or the advice of a health professional or dietician but rather an intuitive feeling they have about their body's ability to tolerate gluten. In one study that followed people who believed they were gluten intolerant for two years, it was determined that 86% of the participants showed no clinical signs of intolerance or sensitivity.

Is this to say that gluten-sensitivity is a made-up phenomenon and that the gluten-free diet industry is opportunistic? The answer is not whether gluten sensitivity is a concept we have imagined. It is very real, and not everyone who is sensitive to gluten will have markers show up on diagnostic tests. To the question that the gluten-free diet industry is opportunistic, well, there is a case to make for that.

I believe that you can be sensitive to gluten, even if you don't present with the classical signs of gluten intolerance. I also feel as though we need to rethink our idea about gluten sensitivity because of the shifting role of gluten in our diets.

Once upon a time, the main sources of gluten came directly from whole grains. As we've embraced a food culture that places processed foods on a pedestal, gluten has found more ways to sneak onto our plates and into our bellies. Gluten isn't just found in whole wheat bread or your favorite high-fiber cereal. Gluten is also added into many processed foods to improve their texture, making them more palatable and appetizing on a mass scale to consumers. The natural sources of gluten have also changed, as new varieties of wheat have a higher gluten content than their predecessors, and grains that are higher in gluten seem to be equipped with natural insecticide qualities.

Combine all of that, with the fact that in the United States, our daily caloric intake is higher than it was a couple of decades ago, assuming that at least some of those extra calories are coming from gluten, and we have a recipe for gluten overload.

We're simply consuming more gluten than we have in the past. Those who might not have noticed a gluten sensitivity a decade ago, are experiencing side effects because the amount of gluten they're consuming is higher than in the past. The more we expose our bodies to an inflammatory trigger, the more likely we are to notice the consequences to our health.

Striking a Balance with Gluten

This part is for those of you who don't have a diagnosed gluten intolerance but are wondering if eliminating gluten from your diet could be the best for your health, and/or the health of your family. First, if you or someone you care for has been diagnosed with gluten intolerance, it's important to eliminate gluten entirely. For certain individuals, gluten can be truly dangerous, and there's no halfway to eating gluten-free.

For the rest of us, it starts with striking a balance with gluten in our lives. You have this book in front of you, so I strongly encourage you to read and absorb each section. Learn as much as you can about gluten and the various ways it can affect your health, especially concerning gut health. Educate yourself on all the places gluten is hiding in your diet, and how even a diet free of packaged and processed foods may still be too high in gluten due to genetic changes in the grains you're consuming.

My goal is to help you with this process and present a plan that eliminates the stress and confusion of transitioning to a gluten-free, or even a reduced-gluten, diet. There is an incredible amount of information out there, some of it more valuable than others. There are also a lot of contradicting opinions out there about gluten and the benefits, or lack of benefits, of eliminating gluten from your diet. My goal here is to cut through all of that for you and present you with a fact-based approach to improving your health. Not everyone will need or want to move to a completely gluten-free diet, but I feel it's important to be aware of the abundance of gluten in the average diet and reduce one's intake as a preventative measure in protecting yourself from gluten-related side effects.

In just a bit, we'll begin going into more detail about the effects of gluten in the body, and why you should work towards balancing your intake of gluten, regardless of if you're currently experiencing any discomfort or side effects when you consume it. Before we get into all these details, and how to reduce your gluten intake, I want to take a minute and go into deeper detail about the different types of gluten-related health issues.

GLUTEN RELATED HEALTH ISSUES

Celiac Disease

Celiac disease is the most severe form of gluten intolerance. Celiac disease is an autoimmune condition that is believed to be genetically influenced, meaning that individuals with a specific genetic marker are more susceptible to developing the disease. While a predisposition to Celiac disease can be inherited, it is thought that a combination of factors, including heredity and environmental triggers, are involved in the development of the disease.

About 95% of people with Celiac disease have the HLA-DQ2 gene. Having this gene doesn't mean that you're destined to develop Celiac disease, but it does mean you're at a greater risk. It is possible to have Celiac disease and not have any relatives that are known to have the condition. Celiac disease affects both men and women, without barriers of age or race.

When a person with Celiac disease consumes gluten, their body responds by initiating an immune response. The immune system attacks the tissues of the small intestine, which damages these little finger-like, vascular projections that line the membrane of the small intestine. These villi are essential for proper nutrient absorption, and when they're repeatedly attacked, your body can no longer absorb nutrients from food the way that it needs to. In the case of undiagnosed Celiac disease, a person may continue to consume gluten, unaware that they're causing severe, long-term damage to their health.

Many of the initial signs of Celiac disease involve some degree of digestive upset. They include:

- Diarrhea
- Constipation
- Bloating
- Gas
- Abdominal pain
- Nausea and/or vomiting
- Weight loss

- Fatigue

As Celiac disease progresses and the small intestine endures more damage, the effects of Celiac disease become more severe. Long term, serious effects associated with Celiac disease include:

- Vitamin and nutrient deficiency
- Anemia
- Nervous system disorders
- Infertility
- Osteoporosis
- Lactose intolerance
- Gallbladder issues
- Seizures
- Dementia
- Neuropathy
- Pancreatic insufficiency

Individuals with Celiac disease also have an increased risk of cardiovascular disease and small bowel cancer. If you have Celiac disease, you are also more at risk of developing other types of autoimmune disorders. A few examples of autoimmune disorders that are associated with Celiac disease include:

- Type I Diabetes
- Grave's Disease (overactive thyroid)
- Hashimoto's Disease (underactive thyroid)

- Systemic Lupus
- Sjogren's Syndrome
- Addison's Disease
- Autoimmune Hepatitis
- Scleroderma

This information regarding the seriousness of Celiac disease is in no way intended to scare you into a gluten-free diet. Currently, only about 1% of people in the United States have been diagnosed with Celiac disease. It is relatively rare, but the numbers seem to be rising. This information provided is to encourage you to seek a diagnosis if you believe you may have Celiac disease and to follow the necessary dietary protocols, such as eliminating gluten, to reduce the severity and long-term effects of the disease.

Non-Celiac Gluten Sensitivity

Non-Celiac gluten sensitivity (NCGS) is a term used to describe a condition where a person experiences many of the same symptoms as someone with Celiac disease but does not meet the clinical definition of the disease. A person with NCGS cannot tolerate gluten in much the same way as someone with Celiac disease, however, they don't show signs of intestinal damage or have the same antibody markers.

A person with NCGS may experience symptoms that are not only uncomfortable but also disruptive to their life. Signs of NCGS may include:

- Abdominal pain/discomfort
- Bloating
- Gas
- Nausea
- Diarrhea
- Constipation
- Chronic inflammation/joint pain
- Headache
- Fatigue
- Brain fog

NCGS affects millions of people in the United States and around the world. It's estimated that the number of people who are living with NCGS is six times greater than the number of people that have been diagnosed with Celiac disease.

We must look at NCGS as a serious health condition that needs to be acknowledged and treated appropriately. While the current thought is that NCGS doesn't cause the type of intestinal damage seen in Celiac disease, the Celiac Disease Foundation quotes a 2016 study confirming that wheat exposure in NCGS may trigger an immune reaction and potentially lead to intestinal damage in some people.

Wheat Allergy

The terms Celiac disease and wheat allergy often commingle even though these two health conditions are very different from one another. Unlike Celiac disease, a person with a wheat allergy isn't responding to the gluten but rather any one of the proteins found in wheat. Gluten is a type of protein, and it's found in wheat but people with Celiac disease or NCGS aren't experiencing an allergic reaction to it.

In the case of a wheat allergy, there's a predictable physiological process that occurs. Any exposure to a potential allergen can trigger your body's antibody response. In the case of allergies, it often takes repeated exposure for the body to identify the allergen as invasive. This is why you might suddenly develop an allergy to something you've been able to tolerate your entire life. Allergies may seem spontaneous but that is rarely the case.

When a person with a wheat allergy consumes the grain, their body releases antibodies, which then attach themselves to mast cells. This leads to a release of histamine in the body, which causes inflammation, swelling, redness, itching, and all the other uncomfortable symptoms of allergies. In the most severe cases, an allergy can become life-threatening.

The common thread between a wheat allergy and gluten intolerance or sensitivity is inflammation. Someone with a wheat allergy may experience a degree of common allergy symptoms, including:

- Hives/rash
- Nasal congestion
- Coughing
- itchy/watery eyes

- nausea/vomiting
- Swelling around the mouth
- Trouble breathing

In addition to these symptoms, someone with a wheat allergy may experience more severe digestive issues. In the case of wheat allergy, it's obvious that you need to avoid wheat, and any foods containing wheat in their list of ingredients. In our world of processed food madness, this can be a real challenge. Individuals with a wheat allergy may also be more sensitive to inflammation in general, and for them, it may be beneficial to reduce or eliminate all types of gluten-containing grains, rather than just wheat alone.

IBS

Irritable Bowel Syndrome (IBS) is an intestinal condition that affects anywhere from 25 to 45 million people in the United States alone. IBS is commonly confused with Inflammatory Bowel Disease, which is an umbrella term that encompasses both Crohn's Disease and Ulcerative Colitis. IBS is considered to be less serious than IBD and is defined as a functional gastrointestinal disorder.

IBS can cause a great deal of comfort and may include symptoms that disrupt your normal, everyday life. IBS doesn't cause long-term, destructive inflammation to the intestines. A person can have both IBS and IBD.

Symptoms of IBS may include:

- Constipation or diarrhea, sometimes both presenting alternately
- Bloating
- Gas
- Abdominal pain
- A sensation of feeling full
- Abdominal swelling
- Mucus when passing stool
- Nausea

Some symptoms that are incorrectly associated with IBS but are more indicative of IBD include the presence of blood in stools, anemia, weight loss, and fever. If you think you have IBS but are experiencing any of these more serious symptoms, it's important to see a health care provider to either diagnose or rule out IBD.

Like many other digestive/gut health disorders, the symptoms of IBS closely mimic those of Celiac disease and NCGS. People with IBS may find that following a gluten-free diet cuts down on inflammation and pain, thereby reducing the severity of their condition. There has also been some interesting research on the connection between IBS and Celiac disease.

It's estimated that about 4% of people with diagnosed IBS also have confirmed Celiac disease. I think this is an interesting statistic because I have to wonder how many physicians who treat patients with IBS actually look for Celiac disease as a coexisting condition. Without research or numbers to back it up, it's hard to say but the symptoms can overlap to the point that Celiac disease may be more likely to go undiagnosed in people with IBS. If you have IBS and are concerned about Celiac disease, I strongly suggest you seek out the advice of a GI specialist that has ample experience not only treating people with Celiac disease but also treating it as a comorbid condition.

Dermatitis Herpetiformis

Dermatitis Herpetiformis is a relatively rare condition that affects individuals with Celiac disease. It's estimated that about 1 in 10,000 people are living with Dermatitis Herpetiformis or DH. For people with DH, the effects of Celiac disease can extend beyond the digestive systems and include sometimes painful, extremely itchy red bumps or blisters on the body.

The cause of DH is the same gluten intolerance that appears in people with digestive symptoms of Celiac disease. While it's common for someone with DH to experience digestive symptoms of Celiac disease, about 20% of individuals with DH will have a normal intestinal biopsy. Even with a normal biopsy and the absence of other markers associated with Celiac disease, a gluten-free diet is the most effective treatment to ease and eliminate symptoms. In some cases, a doctor may prescribe medications that help in alleviating the painful itching and redness associated with the condition.

CHAPTER SUMMARY

In this chapter, we've become better acquainted with gluten, what it is, and what -if anything - is so bad about it. Gluten doesn't affect everyone the same, making it important to take an individual approach to eliminate or reduce it in your diet. What we have discussed specifically in this chapter is:

- How gluten is a term for different types of protein that are found primarily in grains;
- In recent years, gluten has gained a lot of notoriety for being a nutritional bad guy;
- Not everyone will benefit equally from going gluten-free - some might not need to make this type of dietary change at all;
- In sensitive individuals, gluten has been implicated as a causative factor in many types of health issues;
- Most people will find at least some benefit in balancing their intake of gluten.

In the next chapter, we're going to take a closer look at how gluten can affect the body, and spend some time exploring the neurological connections between, gluten, gut health, and the brain.

2

THE EFFECT OF GLUTEN ON YOUR BODY AND MIND

One of the most challenging things about understanding gluten intolerance is that it can manifest itself in many different ways. Symptoms can be different from person to person, but they are also different depending on the type of gluten intolerance or sensitivity someone has.

We've come a long way in understanding the effect of gluten on our health but there is still much we can learn. For instance, it has only been in recent years that we've really started looking at the neurological effects of gluten and expanding our understanding beyond the digestive symptoms.

To complicate our understanding of gluten-related health issues, there are a group of symptoms that occur in people who have Celiac disease and those who have other conditions, like a wheat allergy, which doesn't involve a reaction to the gluten itself. Nausea and vomiting are common symptoms that occur in both conditions but are also fairly common in people with non-Celiac gluten sensitivity and a range of other health issues.

I want to start this section by going into more detail about the most common symptoms of gluten intolerance. Most of these symptoms apply to Celiac disease but many of them also carry over to other gluten-related health issues.

COMMON SYMPTOMS OF GLUTEN INTOLERANCE

Bloating

Bloating is an uncomfortable condition that has no single known cause. Instead, it's associated with a long list of health issues, ranging from minor to severe. Mostly everyone has experienced "feeling bloated" in their life and is familiar with the uncomfortable feeling of fullness and how your clothes suddenly feel tighter.

For most people, bloating has a minor cause and quickly passes. Others experience bloating more frequently, and it's in these cases that it's most important to look at the possible underlying cause. Bloating is one of the primary symptoms of Celiac disease and non-Celiac gluten sensitivity.

Bloating seems to be common in the majority of cases of people with both suspected and diagnosed NCGS. In one study, in particular, bloating was listed as a symptom in 87% of cases of NCGS, beating out abdominal pain, which was reported by 83% of the study participants.

Diarrhea and Constipation

Changes in digestive function are one of the key signals that something isn't quite right in your gut. Everyone experiences the occasional bout of diarrhea or constipation, usually caused by triggers such as stress, dietary changes, or minor illness. Because these symptoms are so relatively common, Celiac disease and NCGS aren't often the first suspected diagnosis.

It is estimated that more than half of people with gluten sensitivity experience diarrhea as the main symptom, while about a quarter of gluten-sensitive individuals deal with chronic bouts of constipation.

In the case of gluten sensitivity or gluten intolerance, exposure to gluten causes an inflammatory response in the small intestine. This inflammation can eventually damage the lining of the intestines and interfere with gut function and healthy gut flora. When these things happen, the stage is set for bowel irregularities, including both diarrhea and constipation.

Abdominal Pain

We've briefly discussed how gluten-related health conditions come with a range of symptoms. For many people with gluten intolerance, the occurrence of abdominal pain is right up there with bloating, diarrhea, and constipation as one of the first and most noticeable symptoms. Abdominal pain that comes with gluten intolerance can range from mild cramping to more intense localized pain that is severe enough to interfere with daily life.

Recurring abdominal pain can have many causes. Infection, inflammation, and intestinal disorders are common culprits. If you've noticed recurring or chronic abdominal pain, a health care provider can help you find the cause. It's also a smart idea to keep a food diary, to help pinpoint any dietary causes, such as gluten.

Headaches

Right about now is when we start getting into the lesser-known symptoms of gluten intolerance. Headaches are one of those things that everyone experiences from time to time, and for many of us, they occur quite frequently. According to the World Health Organization, 1 in 20 adults experiences a headache every single day.

It's no big surprise that tension is one of the leading causes of headaches, but that alone doesn't account for all the headaches we collectively suffer from every day. When checking off the boxes of issues that might be causing your chronic headaches, gluten might not even make it onto your radar.

Chronic headaches are often a main indicator of Celiac disease and gluten-sensitivity. One study that looked at a small group of only 500 participants noted that 30% of people with Celiac disease reported chronic headaches. That number escalates to 56% for study participants with a known gluten sensitivity. This is only one of many bodies of research that connect headaches and migraines to gluten-related health issues.

If you're suffering from frequent headaches and haven't yet entirely cut gluten from your life, I strongly urge you to keep a food diary to help track any connection between diet and your symptoms.

Fatigue

Fatigue is something that seems to be plaguing our society, in general, these days. We're too busy, too stressed, and our bodies aren't always receiving the nutritional fuel they need to run at optimal speed.

The feeling of fatigue is also one of the tools your body uses when it's trying to tell you that something isn't right. When something is going on in your body, whether it's an illness, injury, allergy, or food intolerance, your body automatically reprioritizes how it uses its energy stores.

Fatigue is a fairly common symptom in individuals with Celiac disease. If we look at research on the most common symptoms of CD, fatigue is frequently reported, and we can estimate that more than 80% of individuals experience noticeable tiredness regularly.

Skin Problems

Aside from bloating, most of the symptoms associated with Celiac disease are invisible, affecting the body internally, rather than externally. Outwardly symptoms aren't often associated with the condition, but skin problems are more common with Celiac disease than people realize. Gluten-related skin symptoms sometimes manifest as a painful skin condition called dermatitis herpetiformis.

Dermatitis herpetiformis can be a stand-alone manifestation of Celiac disease, or it can accompany digestive symptoms. Dermatitis herpetiformis can be a troubling symptom of Celiac disease because only about 10% of individuals with these skin symptoms show signs of the digestive symptoms as well. Anytime a symptom falls outside of those we associate with a condition, in this case, Celiac disease, it tends to lengthen the time to receive a proper diagnosis.

Dermatitis herpetiformis isn't the only skin-related manifestation of Celiac disease. Some individuals break out in itchy hives, swollen welts, and lesions. Hives, also called urticaria, is a common skin-related allergic reaction. In the case of Celiac disease, it's suspected that vitamin deficiency could be behind the reason why some people experience urticaria. Other skin conditions related to gluten intolerance may include psoriasis and alopecia areata, which is a type of hair loss that affects between .7% and 3.8% of Celiac patients.

Depression and Anxiety

Depression and anxiety disorders are the most common types of mental illness in the United States. Current numbers suggest that 40 million adults, or about 18% of the population, suffer from these conditions. Considering the stigma around mental health disorders, and a general lack of access to mental health services, we can estimate that this number is actually higher.

Depression and anxiety have many different causes. If you've been experiencing symptoms of anxiety or depression, I urge you to speak to your healthcare provider to help you find a solution. There is help for you, and you don't have to suffer in silence.

Finding the root source of depression and anxiety is key to knocking them out of your life. Medications work for some people and can be very valuable for treatment. However, in many cases, medications should be looked at as a short-term solution to depression and anxiety. It's surprising to me how often we experience these types of mental health issues without knowing that they're manifestations of something else going on in our bodies.

Digestive issues in general have a strong connection to anxiety and depression. Studies have found a higher incidence of anxiety and depression in individuals who have known food allergies, or other types of digestive issues, such as IBS. Considering the level of intestinal damage that Celiac can cause, the connection between gluten intolerance and mental health becomes clearer.

There is a delicate microbiome that exists, and even the slightest disturbance in this microbiome can have an immediate impact on your health. With Celiac disease, a disturbance in this microbiome increases the risk of bad gut bacteria becoming overpopulated. This can affect the central nervous system, which has a direct impact on neurological processes, including those that can lead to depression and anxiety.

Unexplained Weight Loss

A gluten-free diet is one that's more often associated with overall positive changes than purely for weight loss, although going gluten-free may help some people focus more on whole, nutrient-dense foods that are lower in fat and calories. However, those with Celiac disease often find that unexplained weight loss is a common symptom.

Celiac disease causes intestinal inflammation. The pain and discomfort alone are enough to interfere with one's appetite and desire to eat, especially before diagnosis when the cause is unknown. The intestinal inflammation of Celiac disease also interferes with nutrient absorption, leading to malnutrition and unintended weight loss.

Anemia

Anemia, which is a condition where the body is lacking in red blood cells to sufficiently carry and deliver oxygen throughout the body, is a known symptom of gluten intolerance. The symptoms of anemia range from fatigue and shortness of breath, to headaches, dizziness, and a rapid heart rate.

For the body to make red blood cells, it needs iron. There are plenty of good (non-gluten) dietary sources of iron. The problem is that the damage caused to the intestinal lining in Celiac disease makes it difficult for the body to absorb what it needs from nutritional sources and oral supplements alone. This results in a significant number of people with Celiac-related impaired intestinal function developing anemia at some point.

Autoimmune Disorders

Celiac disease is an autoimmune disorder, meaning that something about gluten causes the body to attack itself. This is just one on a long list of autoimmune disorders that together affect more than 23 million people in the United States.

It isn't quite known why but individuals with one autoimmune disorder are more at risk of developing additional autoimmune disorders at some point in their lives. This seems to be especially true in the case of Celiac disease.

When looking at a sampling of the most common autoimmune disorders, Celiac disease presents itself as a coexisting condition in a notable number of cases. Celiac disease is thought to be present in up to 19% of individuals with type I diabetes, up to 5% in individuals with autoimmune thyroid disorders, and a notable number of individuals with autoimmune liver disease and inflammatory bowel disease.

Brain Fog

We all have those days when our brains feel sluggish and it's impossible to concentrate on anything. This feeling of hazy, clouded thinking is affectionately referred to as brain fog, and it's one of those things that everyone deals with from time to time.

If you're finding that you're having difficulty concentrating, thinking, or just feel "mentally" tired more often than not, gluten intolerance may be to blame. For those who are intolerant or sensitive, gluten can have neurological effects.

The jury is still out on why brain fog is common in people with gluten-related health issues, but we can take a few educated guesses here. For starters, we know that in sensitive individuals, gluten can interfere with nutrient absorption and increase the risk of anemia. When your body isn't getting what it needs from a nutritional standpoint, mental capabilities are going to suffer. You're going to feel tired and lack energy. This is sure to carry over to mental fitness as well.

Secondly, it's stressful to not feel well. It's stressful to know, or at least suspect, that something is wrong with your body.

Gluten-related health issues, both severe and mild, can leave you focused on something other than the task at hand. Worrying about your health or not feeling well can also disrupt your sleep habits, further exaggerating any brain fog that you might have.

Muscle Pain

The symptoms of gluten intolerance involve inflammation. Because gluten is something we ingest, we tend to think of that inflammatory response as being confined to the gut, but this isn't the case. Many people with gluten intolerance experience symptoms of chronic inflammation throughout their body, including their muscles and joints.

People with gluten intolerance might suffer from chronic or occasional muscle and joint pain in their back, shoulders, knees, hips, and other joint areas that are commonly affected by systemic inflammation.

Mood Swings

Are you happy one minute and snapping at the people around you the next? Maybe you start the day feeling optimistic but by lunchtime, you feel like throwing in the towel and heading back to bed. We've all been there but for people with gluten-related health issues, every day can feel like an emotional roller coaster.

This side effect of gluten intolerance is another one that still isn't completely understood. With mood swings, there also exists the problem that we so often feel like we need to suck it up and put on a steady exterior for those around us. Mood swings can be blamed on lack of sleep, stress, and several other causes that make it all too easy to just brush off this common symptom.

Inflammation and insufficient nutrient absorption can both be precursors to excessive mood swings. For example, tryptophan is an essential amino acid that the body cannot synthesize on its own, so it must be obtained from dietary sources. Tryptophan has different roles, including the regulation of sleep and mood. If intestinal damage from gluten exposure makes it more difficult for the body to absorb tryptophan, mood swings become a natural consequence.

Dental Problems

Dental problems are among the lesser-known but serious symptoms of gluten intolerance. Dental health is often an indicator of one's overall health, making it important to pay close attention to any changes you or your dentist notice.

Gluten intolerance can affect the production of two proteins that are essential for oral health - enamelin and amelogenin. These proteins are essential for the regeneration of enamel, which protects your teeth from acid and eventually decay.

We also see nutrient absorption enter the picture again here. Gluten can interfere with the body's ability to absorb certain nutrients that are needed for strong and healthy teeth and gums.

As a result, people with gluten-related health issues tend to suffer from more dental problems than the average person.

IS IT ALL IN YOUR HEAD? THE NEUROLOGICAL EFFECTS OF GLUTEN

One of the biggest challenges in learning to recognize the effects of gluten is the general perception that symptoms of gluten sensitivity or intolerance manifest only in the gut. We've just covered a fairly extensive list of some of the symptoms and side effects experienced by gluten-sensitive individuals. You can see from that list that gluten doesn't discriminate regarding where and how it impacts your health.

While awareness of Celiac disease and NCGS has increased in recent years, our understanding of the full scope of the impact on one's health hasn't. One area where this is most evident is our understanding, and acceptance, of the neurological effects of gluten in sensitive individuals.

Science has been looking at the connection between gluten and neurological effects for decades at this point, but it still remains less of an area of focus than it should. One of the things that I find most interesting is that in Celiac disease, it's often digestive related symptoms that provide the first clues to a gluten-related issue. In people with NCGS, where the body responds differently to gluten than in Celiac disease, it's often neurological issues that offer the first warning signs.

Recent data suggests that nearly a quarter of people with Celiac disease develop some degree of neurological issues or psychiatric dysfunction. The same body of research that reveals this data also says that more than 57% of people with neurological issues of unknown origin test positive for anti-gliadin antibodies. We also know people with NCGS frequently test positive for gliadin antibodies. There's an obvious connection here between gliadin antibodies and neurological processes.

The range of neurological issues experienced by people with Celiac disease and NCGS is expansive. Reported symptoms range from occasional, although sometimes debilitating, migraines, to depression, anxiety, ADHD, memory loss, and schizophrenia. We need to remember that neurological disorders affect the entire body. Someone with depression may experience fatigue and a very real pain in their muscles and joints. Neuropathy presents with weakness, numbness, and pain that affects primarily hands and feet. We don't always think of these things as having a neurological connection, but they do, and a person's sensitivity to gluten can play a major role in the development and severity of these types of conditions.

Gluten's Three Pathways to Neurological Damage

I think it's important to take some time here and discuss what happens beyond the digestive system when a sensitive person ingests gluten. The body's efficiency always amazes me. Even in the case of gluten sensitivity, where there is this incredible range of potential symptoms, the biological processes that cause these reactions are pretty straightforward.

In gluten sensitivity, some things happen that alter the activity of the gut-brain axis. The gut-brain axis? Yes, this is a real term and it represents bidirectional communication that occurs between the central nervous system and the gut's enteric nervous system.

Whenever you hear how gut health is important to overall health, this gut-brain axis is directly involved. There is strong evidence to suggest the quality of the gut microbiome plays a key role in nervous system interactions that occur along the gut-brain axis. When inflammation occurs, with or without the intestinal damage that is a known factor in Celiac disease, the microbiome is altered, and this opens up multiple pathways for gluten to interfere with neurological processes.

People with Celiac disease and NCGS both experience neurological symptoms from gluten and are at a greater risk for the three different ways that gluten can damage the neurological system. Here, we're going to take a closer look at each of these pathways.

Cross-Reactivity

The first pathway I want to discuss is cross-reactivity. The simplest way to describe cross-reactivity is to say that the body isn't always capable of differentiating between healthy nerve tissue and gluten, so it attacks both. It sounds a bit crazy but there is enough molecular mimicry between nervous system proteins and the gluten troublemaker, gliadin, that the body's immune response feverishly attacks both.

Molecular mimicry is thought to be the main factor in the development of autoimmune conditions, at least in those that are a response to infectious agents or chemical exposure. There is currently some very interesting research underway that looks at autoreactive T cells in response to molecular mimicry, in hopes of better understanding autoimmune disease, along with how we can treat or even prevent it. This could lead to hopeful findings for individuals who are living with Celiac disease and other autoimmune conditions.

Going back to the cross-reactivity and the neurological effects of gluten sensitivity, every time gluten is ingested, the body attacks not only the gluten proteins but also nerve and brain tissue. This is one of the body's more dangerous responses to gluten because it has the potential to destroy and permanently damage neurological tissues.

Transglutaminase 6 Reactivity

Transglutaminase 6 reactivity is a mouthful, so we're going to shorten it to TG6 reactivity. This response is similar to cross-reactivity in that gluten triggers an immune response to TG6. This is problematic because the TG6 enzyme helps the body digest wheat, which is one of the main sources of gluten. TG6 is also responsible for binding other types of proteins.

When the body initiates an immune response to TG6, transglutaminase 6 antibodies are produced. One study showed TG6 antibodies to be present in 73% of individuals with gluten ataxia, which is a condition marked by loss of balance, loss of coordination, difficulty speaking, gross motor skill difficulties, and tingling in the extremities, caused by a reaction to gluten. A high prevalence of TG6 antibodies also exists in individuals with gluten-related neuropathy.

TG6 reactivity occurs in some people with gluten sensitivity but it's currently unclear what percentage of individuals are affected. When a sensitive person consumes gluten, there is a reaction that occurs in the digestive system, which can also serve as a trigger to attack TG6 at points of the nervous system.

Leaky Blood-Brain Barrier

The third mechanism through which gluten leads to neurological damage is by creating a leaky blood-brain barrier. If you're thinking that this sounds like a premise for a horror movie, I agree. When we talk about the blood-brain barrier, we're referring to a protective border that's composed of endothelial cells (cells that line the interior of both lymphatic and blood vessels).

The blood-brain barrier is semi-permeable, but the endothelial cells are highly selective in what they allow to pass through. When this barrier is functioning as it should, it allows the passage of nutrients, water, amino acids, glucose, and other molecules that are critical to proper neural function. In addition to regulating what passes through to the brain, this barrier also keeps out all the harmful stuff that may interfere with neurological function.

To me, this is one of the most interesting elements of the effect of gluten on neurological function. The inflammatory effects of gluten, especially in sensitive individuals, affect the blood-brain barrier just the same as in the gut, and other areas of the body. It's this inflammation that begins to break down the blood-brain barrier, causing it to lose some functional efficiency. This means that harmful substances can pass through the barrier and into the previously off-limits environment of the brain. From this point, the potential effects on neurological health are expansive.

What I find interesting is that science is beginning to make connections between gluten and many different types of neurological disorders, which we'll cover in more detail in the next section. I want to say this now, and I will without a doubt repeat it several times in the next section, that we have limited, if any proof that gluten plays a role in instigating some of the neurological conditions we're about to discuss. However, considering what we do know about gluten and the proven neurological effects, we can begin having educated discussions on the implications of gluten in some of the more common neurological disorders we see today.

Neurological Disorders with Potential Links to Gluten-Related Conditions

The question we're facing today isn't "if" gluten affects the neurological system but rather the degree of damage it can cause, and the potential neurological outcomes of repeated exposure. We already know that gluten can cause a range of neurological symptoms from brain fog and migraines, to neuropathy and ataxia. Science has supplied us with decades of research and studies that confirm all of this.

What we have less of is scientific evidence to support gluten's role in more serious neurological conditions, such as bipolar disorder, autism, ADHD, epilepsy, or schizophrenia. These neurological conditions have proven relentlessly difficult for scientists to pinpoint a cause. In so many cases, it's impossible to look at two people living with the same neurological illness and find a common contributing link between them.

I'd like to take some time and discuss a few neurological conditions individually, including the possible role of gluten in sensitive individuals with these conditions. At this point, we still don't know who may or may not be affected by gluten in these ways but looking closer at these conditions can provide an interesting perspective and reason to consider eliminating gluten from your life.

Depression and Anxiety

Depression and anxiety affect millions of people in the United States. Any type of chronic health issue is by its very nature likely to increase the risk of depression and anxiety. Celiac disease and NCGS aren't an exception to this but we're starting to see that people with these gluten-related conditions might be at a greater risk of depression and anxiety than the general population.

To connect a symptom like depression or anxiety to a gluten-related health issue, we have to ask the question of why. Why are people with these conditions at a greater risk of depression and anxiety, and is the increased risk based on anything more than the emotional factors of living with any type of disease? In all honesty, we don't have concrete evidence as to why this seems to be the case. What we do have are researchers who are investigating the possibility that disturbances in nutritional absorption that eventually lead to nutritional deficiencies may be at least partially to blame.

The B vitamin family provides a clear model of how nutritional deficiencies may contribute to depression and anxiety in people with gluten-related health issues. B vitamins have been linked to neurological function, with deficiencies being connected to neurological disorders. Concerning depression and anxiety, vitamins B1, B3, B6, B9, and B12 are crucial. If the body isn't able to fully absorb these nutrients due to inflammation or intestinal damage, this creates an environment where depressive symptoms may begin to manifest.

The type of intestinal damage that leads to these types of nutritional deficiencies is found primarily in individuals with Celiac disease and not those with NCGS. A second theory that more fully addresses why individuals with NCGS also experience higher rates of depression and anxiety focuses more on how gluten disrupts the gut microbiome and how that in turn interferes with the processes of the gut-brain axis.

Insomnia, ADHD, and Brain Fog

I realize that this category may seem a little random, but I want to focus for a minute on how insomnia, ADHD, and brain fog are interconnected, at least in the context of a reaction to gluten. I've witnessed in my own practice that distraction, brain fog, and insomnia all seem to go hand in hand, especially when gluten shows itself as the culprit.

I want to clarify that ADHD is a serious issue on its own and is a disruptive force in many people's lives. I have included it here because the defining characteristics of problems focusing, restlessness, hyperactivity, agitation, forgetfulness, and mood variations all fit in the spectrum of neurological issues that are suspected to occur as a result of gluten exposure in some people.

I think it's safe to say that each of us experience brain fog, the inability to focus, and the occasional bout of insomnia. What I've witnessed in my practice is the point of near desperation that people reach when these issues become defining themes in their lives. I've personally witnessed how eliminating gluten can provide relief of these symptoms.

However, I'm not one to ask you to take my anecdotal evidence and make lifelong changes based on it. We're still waiting for science to catch up with us here regarding the effects of gluten on these areas of cognitive function but there have been some studies that are paving the way. For example, a handful of studies have found that symptoms of ADHD appear to be overrepresented in individuals with Celiac disease. An additional report mentions that in patients with Celiac disease, following a gluten-free diet significantly improved symptoms of ADHD.

At the end of the day, we know that gluten produces neurological symptoms, which often include brain fog and insomnia, along with the key indicators of ADHD. It's worth considering if adopting a gluten-free diet could be therapeutic for individuals living with these conditions.

Migraines

Migraines are an unfortunate fact of life for many people. Migraines, in general, are poorly understood. There seems to be a mixture of genetic and environmental factors that puts a person at a higher risk of experiencing migraines in their lifetime, but the exact formula is still elusive. There is often a triggering factor that initiates a migraine but even those vary among sufferers. For some people it's stress. For others, it might be hormonal changes, environmental changes, physical exertion, medications, food, sensory stimuli...the list goes on and on.

We do have some insight into what might be causing migraines in a certain group of people, more specifically, those with Celiac disease or NCGS. People with these conditions seem to suffer from migraines disproportionately compared to the general population.

Studies indicate that about 25% of people with NCGS report chronic headaches and migraines. Additional data points to about 30% of individuals with Celiac disease reporting chronic headaches or migraines. The majority of this 30% describe their headaches as severe, compared to lower numbers in individuals with other types of autoimmune disorders.

Peripheral Neuropathy

Earlier, when we were discussing the three main ways that gluten can affect neurological function, we touched on molecular mimicry with gluten and how this can damage the nervous system. This is just one mechanism through which it is believed that gluten exposure leads to a condition called peripheral neuropathy.

According to an article published by the University of Chicago Celiac Disease Center, neuropathy is one of the most common reported symptoms of Celiac disease. Neuropathy is generally described as a malfunction of the peripheral nerves. Symptoms of this vary widely but for people with Celiac disease, the most common manifestations are pain, tingling, and numbness, especially in the hands and feet. General muscle weakness is also reported but at a lower incidence.

In addition to molecular mimicry, nutritional deficiencies are also suspected in the presence of neuropathy in individuals with gluten-related health issues. Deficiencies of vitamins B12, B6, and E are suggested to play critical roles.

The final theory is that we know people with Celiac disease are more likely to develop at least one other autoimmune disorder, for which neuropathy may be a symptom of. If you're experiencing the symptoms of neuropathy, it's important to speak with a health professional to determine the cause. Eliminating gluten from your diet and supplementing with vitamins that play a key role in neuropathy should be considered as complementary therapy while working towards a diagnosis.

Epilepsy and Vertigo

Epilepsy and vertigo, while not connected, are two of the lesser reported potential effects of gluten intolerance or sensitivity. I want to refer to the above section on neuropathy as to the different ways gluten can affect the nervous system and lead to a range of symptoms, including vertigo, and in more extreme cases, epilepsy.

Vertigo is that feeling of the ground below you being a little off-kilter. You might experience it as dizziness, lack of balance, or a spinning sensation. Vertigo is fairly common, and the incidence tends to increase as we age. It's almost always short-lived and in the majority of cases related to something going on in the middle ear. The common cold is a frequent culprit in mild vertigo.

There are other types of vertigo, such as positional vertigo, where a sudden shift in position can create an immediate but short-lived sensation of being off-balance. There are also other causes of vertigo, including a condition called Meniere's disease, which may be linked in some cases to Celiac disease and wheat allergies. The Gluten-Free Society references a study in which nearly 57% of patients with Meniere's disease tested positive for gliadin sensitivity.

Epilepsy is another neurological condition caused by malfunctions in electrical activity that occurs in the brain. Neurons are misfiring, which leads to seizures. Like so many neurological conditions, the true roots of epilepsy are still largely not understood. For some, genetics plays a role. For others, injury, infection, or environmental factors are to blame.

Celiac disease or gluten sensitivity isn't widely supported as a cause of epilepsy, at least currently. However, there are some interesting investigations into a connection between Celiac disease, bilateral occipital calcifications, and seizures in a condition called CEC syndrome, where a gluten-free diet is prescribed as an element of treatment.

Schizophrenia and Bipolar Disorder

I find the association between gluten and mental health disorders such as schizophrenia and bipolar disorder to be incredibly interesting. First, there is such a tremendous amount of stigma attached to these conditions. This is a generalization that certainly doesn't apply to everyone but society as a whole tends to group serious mental health disorders into this neat little box where they never really get looked at, acknowledged, or understood.

It would be walking on a fine line to say that schizophrenia and bipolar disorder are the faults of gluten. Obviously, there are plenty of examples where this isn't the case. Yet again, there is so much about these conditions that we just don't understand. Our knowledge needs to expand exponentially before we'll reach a point where we can identify not only the root cause but also treatments and solutions.

This idea isn't exactly aligned with the mental health medical community which holds firm to the idea that schizophrenia and bipolar disorder aren't curable. Instead, they're treated with handfuls of pharmaceuticals as everyone hopes for the best. In the case of bipolar disorder, medications have proven to be overall ineffective in managing the condition. This leaves people with these conditions feeling broken, useless, and hopeless. A gluten-free diet isn't going to help everyone that suffers from these conditions, but we've seen some pretty convincing research that it may be helpful to some.

The link between gluten sensitivity and schizophrenia has been studied for much longer than most of us realize. Reports go back as far as the 1950s, examining a connection between the pathogenesis of schizophrenia and a sensitivity to gluten proteins. Seventy years of looking at this connection and still not having it more clearly defined are frustrating, to say the least.

We're looking at decades of studies from all over the world, some of which show a clear connection. For example, a study that looked at the prevalence of Celiac disease before the onset of schizophrenic symptoms, and another that looked at an increased incidence of schizophrenia in individuals with at least one known autoimmune disorder. NCGS has also been implicated as being a cofactor in the onset of psychosis and schizophrenia.

Bipolar disorder is what was formerly referred to as manic depressive illness, and is characterized by notable shifts in mood, attention span, and energy levels. There are several types of bipolar disorder, defined primarily by the severity, frequency, and duration of manic episodes. There is an emerging connection between inflammation and bipolar disorder, and the potential role of gluten in facilitating an abnormal, inflammatory immune response.

Other studies have noted that levels of gluten antibodies are higher in individuals when they are experiencing a bipolar manic episode. Gluten intolerance as causation for bipolar disorder hasn't been established, and we can't say at this time whether it ever will be. However, there is strong enough evidence to support the idea of a gluten-free diet being therapeutic for individuals who are living with bipolar disorder.

Autoimmune Brain Damage

Autoimmune brain damage is a seldom discussed consequence of autoimmune disease. It's one of those topics that you don't hear about or discuss until you find yourself in a situation where it might impact your life directly. Autoimmune brain damage occurs when the body's immune system over responds and attacks normal, healthy tissue of the brain or spinal cord, the same way that it may attack other tissues in the body. The resulting inflammation and damage can lead to neurological symptoms.

People with Celiac disease, where the body produces an autoimmune response, are at risk of a condition called gluten ataxia. Gluten ataxia is the formal term for damage caused to brain and spinal tissues as a result of gluten exposure in intolerant individuals.

Gluten ataxia can affect speech, balance, movement, and posture. Symptoms can range from mild to severe in people with Celiac disease with no clear indication as to why one person may be affected more severely than another. Fortunately, the number of people with Celiac disease who suffer from autoimmune brain damage is believed to be relatively small. However, there also exists the possibility that individuals with ataxia of unknown origin may, in fact, have a gluten sensitivity. If this were discovered to be true, it would increase the relative numbers of Celiac disease patients with this condition.

Unfortunately, some of the symptoms of autoimmune brain damage can't be reversed. The brain is an incredible organ, and research into neuroplasticity has provided intriguing insights into the brain's ability to heal itself. Still, it is generally assumed that brain damage is permanent. A person with gluten ataxia can stop damage in its tracks by making the shift to a completely gluten-free diet.

Autism

Autism is a topic of tremendous debate. There is no shortage of theories surrounding the causes of autism, and it's a subject that many people feel very passionate about. An interesting bit of data regarding autism is the degree to which incidence has grown. Of course, some of this can be attributed to better diagnostic tools and parents who are more likely to seek a diagnosis than those from previous decades. According to the CDC, the prevalence of autism in 2000 was 1 in 150 children. By the year 2016, that number was 1 in 54. These numbers represent diagnoses ranging along the autism spectrum.

Any way you look at it, this is an incredible spike in prevalence in just 16 years. Concerning gluten-sensitivity, research isn't pointing toward gluten as causing autism but rather that autism may be present in the range of gluten-sensitivity symptoms. In other words, gluten hasn't been implicated as a causative factor but there is enough evidence to suggest that dysfunctional gut-brain axis activity may play a role in some cases. The same breakdown of the gut-brain axis that is present in people with NCGS has also been shown to be a characteristic of autism.

Earlier, we talked about the deterioration of the blood-brain barrier that occurs in people who are intolerant of gluten. This deterioration has been implicated in behavioral changes that are aligned with those seen in autism. Interestingly, in children that have been diagnosed with autism, we're seeing higher gliadin antibodies, which also forges a connection between autism spectrum disorders and gluten sensitivity.

CHAPTER SUMMARY

In this chapter, we've seen that the effects of gluten aren't confined to just the gut. What happens in the gut directly affects other areas of your body, including immune function and neurological processes. Many people suffer from neurological symptoms of gluten intolerances, including anxiety, depression, and possibly autism. What we have discussed in this chapter is:

- Gluten intolerance can manifest itself in many different ways;
- Symptoms of gluten intolerance range from digestive upset to neurological and mood disorders;

- There is a physiological connection between the gut and neurological processes;
- There are three main pathways that gluten follows to impact neurological function.

In the next chapter, we're going to explore the intricate relationship between gluten and the gut, along with what it all means for your health.

3

GLUTEN AND THE GUT: ARE THEY MORTAL ENEMIES?

When discussing a gluten-free lifestyle with my clients, I'm sometimes asked if gluten and the gut are destined to be mortal enemies. The answer to this question is complex, and includes yes, no, and maybe.

For people with gluten-intolerance, as is present in Celiac disease, the answer is, without a doubt, yes. In these individuals, exposure to gluten can become a very dangerous situation. There is no getting around the fact that gluten and the digestive system were not meant to be on friendly terms in this case.

Then there are the people with NCGS, along with those who don't present with any of the clinical markers of gluten-sensitivity but understand their body well enough to know that something isn't right when they consume gluten. Gluten sensitivity can present in several ways and vary in severity. Some people might be fine eating small amounts of gluten or consuming select gluten-containing grains. Others in this category won't have the same wiggle room. For these people, the answer ranges from maybe to yes.

Then, some people seem to be relatively unaffected by gluten. They really are out there, and for these people, gluten doesn't present a problem. Something about their physiology protects them from developing the same gluten-related issues that we see in sensitive or intolerant people. For them, the answer is no, at least for now. Gluten-related health issues can suddenly appear, even in individuals without a known history of issues with gluten.

I know that a lot of you out there already have understood that your body and gluten just aren't a good match. I also know that others are seeking information about how gluten impacts your health. Maybe some of you aren't concerned about your own health as much as you are about a child, partner, family member, or friend that seems to be struggling with their body's reaction to gluten.

What I've found in much of the literature I've personally read is that there is an incredible amount of information to support that gluten isn't the best thing for gut health. In some cases, it becomes dangerous to a person's overall health. I hold firm to the belief that knowledge is power, especially when it comes to improving and protecting one's health.

The issue I'm having is that you're being told an awful lot about why gluten is bad for your gut but aren't being provided with a foundation of knowledge, beyond the basics, in what the digestive system is and how it works.

It's impossible to put together a puzzle when you're missing pieces. Knowing how the digestive system functions is just as important as understanding why gluten presents such a challenge. My goal in this section is to help you better understand the digestive system, beyond what you might have learned in elementary school. We don't need to get into a college-level physiology lesson lecture on the digestive system here, but I do think it's important to have a solid base of knowledge.

THE DIGESTIVE SYSTEM: WHAT IT IS AND HOW IT WORKS

The digestive system is one of your body's organ systems. It is made up of a group of organs that all have crucial roles in the digestive process. The central components of the digestive system are referred to as the gastrointestinal (GI) tract. This is where all the digestive action happens. The GI tract includes everything that food passes through, from the first bite until it is eliminated. This includes the mouth, esophagus, stomach, both the large and small intestines, and the rectum. This is where food is digested or broken down, and where nutrients are absorbed.

The digestive system also includes other organs that play key roles in digestion, nutrient absorption, and nutrient synthesis. The gallbladder, pancreas, and liver are all considered part of the digestive system.

When we're talking about the digestive system concerning gluten-related health issues, we're primarily speaking of the "gut" or GI tract. The gallbladder, pancreas, and liver certainly play vital roles and may suffer the effects of inflammation or hormone fluctuations caused by the body's response to gluten. However, the initial point of contact, where the first signs of damage occur, is in the gut.

The process of digestion seems pretty straight forward. You eat, the food makes its way to your stomach where digestive juices begin to break it down. Soon after, the broken-down food moves through the small and large intestines, which serve as a final point of nutrient absorption before the body begins to process the leftovers as waste.

What many people don't understand about their digestive systems is how complex the gut is. Once food is partially broken down by the stomach, it then passes into the small intestines. The small intestine is a narrow digestive tube that measures about 22 feet in the average adult. For the average-sized person that is at least 3.5 times the length of their body. Each bite you take has a lot of traveling to do.

The small intestine is divided into three separate segments. The first is the duodenum, which is the part of the small intestine that is connected to the stomach. It extends from the stomach, around the pancreas in a C-shape form. The jejunum is the central part of the small intestines, and the ileum is the final stretch that connects to your colon or large intestine. When looking at a diagram of human anatomy, the small intestine is what appears to be a swirling mass of tubing in the center of your abdomen.

The majority of the food you eat is digested by the small intestine and this is where nutrient absorption takes place. The small intestines are lined with these minuscule, finger-like structures called villi. Villi are large enough to be seen without a microscope but so incredibly small that you wouldn't immediately notice them if you didn't know what you were looking for. On the larger end of a spectrum, the average villus (the single form of villa) isn't any taller than the thickness of a line made with a fine tip pen. Some are even smaller.

The role of the villi is to absorb nutrients so that they can be synthesized by your body most efficiently. The surface area of the villi is important because the more surface area you have, the more nutrients you can absorb. Think of the amount of water you can absorb with a large sponge you might use to wash your car, compared to the small one sitting next to the kitchen sink. When it comes to absorption, surface area matters.

When the intestinal villa is healthy, you have about a football field's worth of surface area that's absorbing nutrients in your small intestines. When this villa is damaged, as in the case of Celiac disease, the surface area is significantly decreased – meaning it becomes exponentially more difficult for your body to absorb all the nutrients it needs. This is where gluten intolerance has one of its first and most significant impacts.

By the time, the food you've eaten makes its way through the small intestine, it is mostly in liquid form and most of the nutrients have been extracted. Now it's time for it to make its way into the first part of the large intestine, which is the caecum, or cecum. The liquidly food waste first passes through something called the ileocecal valve as it makes its way into the large intestine. The primary purpose of the large intestine is to absorb water and minerals, which helps to solidify the food waste and prepare it to pass through the remainder of the colon where it can be expelled.

There's a children's book titled *"Everyone Poops"*. What we've just described is a grown-up version of that book. In a healthy digestive system, food enters and makes its way out in a rather uneventful fashion. The digestive system is hard at work but it's so efficient that you barely notice it doing its job. It's only when problems arise, such as those associated with gluten intolerance or sensitivity, that we realize just how easily something can go wrong and serious the effects can be.

NEGATIVE EFFECTS OF GLUTEN IN THE GUT

Now that we've covered the basic anatomy and physiology of the digestive system, we can look more closely at how gluten affects it. The thing about gluten is that it doesn't affect everyone the same way. Some people experience severe reactions while others can consume gluten for years, barely noticing any negative effects at all.

Here, I want to talk about three different ways that gluten negatively affects gut health. As we're discussing this, I want you to keep in mind that your individual situation is just that - individual. The effects talked about here might resonate strongly with you, or you might not be able to connect your own symptoms to them at all. I hope that with a better understanding of the digestive system functions, you're able to understand the potential scope of each way gluten affects the gut more fully, regardless of what your individual symptoms are.

Altering the Gut's Microbiome

The first area I want to cover is one that has already been mentioned a couple of times earlier in this book. Gluten has a way of altering the gut's microbiome, and not for the better.

What is the gut's microbiome, you ask? Well, you have an insanely large community of microbial helpers that live in your digestive tract. This community includes bacteria, eukarya, and archaea (all little microorganisms), in numbers that are almost impossible to imagine. These microorganisms help keep the digestive tract functioning properly. They protect against intestinal pathogens, help build immunity, play a role in synthesizing energy, and so much more. They truly are little powerhouses.

In a healthy gut microbiome, there is a mixture of good microorganisms and bad, just like you'd find in any society. To keep things functioning properly, the good guys need to outnumber the bad – again, just like in any society. It's all a delicate balance but for the most part, there's harmony, and the microbiome can flourish and carry out its duties.

That is until something comes along and disrupts the balance of the gut's microbiome. Illness and antibiotics are two examples of forces that can prove to be destructive to the microbiome. In most cases, these disturbances are short-lived and easily remedied. The true problem occurs when you have a chronic issue that disrupts the balance, effectively disabling the microbiome from carrying out its duties. Gluten intolerance is an example of such a disruptor.

I want to mention that any food you eat can have a positive or negative effect on your gut's microbiome. For example, foods that are high in processed sugars feed bad bacteria while foods that are high in fiber feed the good bacteria.

What we're learning is that there's much more to balancing the gut's microbiome than previously suspected. Certain foods, even when they're otherwise thought to be healthy for gut bacteria can alter the microbiome in such a way that its effectiveness is diminished. This is appearing to be the case with gluten.

Research has compared the contents of the gut microbiome in patients with Celiac disease to those in people with no known CD present. What they've found is that the population of harmful bacteria is significantly higher in patients with Celiac disease, where the population of good bacteria is lower. This throws off the balance and opens the door of gastrointestinal symptoms and side effects. Keep in mind that the gut-brain axis is also highly dependent on a balanced, functioning gut microbiome. Without the right balance, a person with Celiac disease also becomes more susceptible to neurological conditions associated with the disease.

Causing Inflammation

Inflammation is the hallmark symptom of every autoimmune disorder, including Celiac disease. In CD and people with wheat allergies, the body produces an immune response and inflammation is the natural consequence. Inflammation has also been shown to be present in people who suffer from NCGS, and not just Celiac disease.

Inflammation is the root of many health issues and is behind practically every serious health condition we see in our society today. Inflammation is involved in heart disease, diabetes, cancer, and the list goes on. Inflammation damages tissue, damages cells, and makes it more difficult for the body to repair itself.

In the case of gluten intolerance, inflammation can be especially dangerous. One of the reasons that gluten-related inflammation is so serious is that it creates an environment where the gut becomes more permeable. This is called leaky gut syndrome, which we'll discuss in more detail in just a moment.

For those who are susceptible to gluten-related inflammation, it's important to consider the consequences of long-term systemic inflammation. In many people, it isn't just the gut that is affected when gluten is consumed. The resulting inflammatory response can affect any of the body's tissues. We discussed in the previous chapter how inflammation plays a role in the neurological effects of gluten intolerance. Inflammation is also why people with Celiac disease and NCGS suffer from joint and muscle pain.

In the environment of the gut, inflammation also makes the gut-brain axis more fragile. Preventing the range of side effects caused by gluten begins with protecting the gut from gluten-related inflammation.

Leaky Gut Syndrome

I want to take a minute and discuss something called leaky gut syndrome. Perhaps you've heard of this, or at least heard the term thrown around here and there. Leaky gut syndrome is a bit of a mystery for the medical community and there are still a sizable number of medical professionals who will go as far as to deny it even exists.

Leaky gut is best described as intestinal permeability. In other words, a degree of damage has occurred to the intestinal tissues and intestinal walls and they're no longer capable of keeping toxins, bacteria, and other foreign substances from entering the bloodstream.

I can't help but look at the medical community's attitude toward leaky gut syndrome and not think of other invisible, mysterious conditions like fibromyalgia and chronic fatigue syndrome. As with these conditions, something serious is going on in the body, and just shrugging one's shoulders because the cause is unknown isn't sufficient.

Signs of leaky gut syndrome may include:

- Bowel abnormalities, such as diarrhea or constipation
- Gassiness and bloating
- Poor nutritional absorption, leading to deficiencies
- Weakened immune system
- Fatigue
- Skin issues, like rashes, acne, or rosacea
- Lack of focus or brain fog
- Headaches
- Inflammatory joining pain
- Mental health issues

- Unusual cravings for sugary or starchy foods
- A known autoimmune disease, such as Celiac disease, Crohn's disease, or rheumatoid arthritis.

What we're learning is that leaky gut may not be a separate condition on its own but rather an indicator that something else is going on - something that is damaging the integrity of the digestive linings.

This is where gluten enters the picture. Gluten is suspected to play a role in leaky gut syndrome because of the damage it can cause in people who are sensitive or intolerant. We've talked about inflammation and also about the irreversible damage that occurs in Celiac disease. Considering this, it's worth looking into the idea that gluten could be behind many of the cases of leaky gut syndrome we're seeing today.

CHAPTER SUMMARY

In this chapter, we've looked at the relationship between gluten and gut health while exploring the ways that gluten can harm and lead to permanent damage of the digestive system. We have specifically discussed:

- The human digestive system is a complex network of several hard-working, important organs;
- The digestive system is resilient but relies on a balance of the gut's microbiome;

- Gluten can disrupt the balance of the gut's microbiome, leading to a domino effect of ill health;
- Gluten can cause gut inflammation and even irreversible damage in people with Celiac disease.

In the next chapter, we're going to move beyond the effects of gluten on the body and look at all the sources of gluten we're exposed to, often in places you'd never suspect.

4

HOW GLUTEN HIDES IN POPULAR FOODS AND PRODUCTS

The first step to eliminating gluten from your life is identifying all the various sources you have in your life. Most people associate gluten with wheat, which is a primary source. Wheat is hidden in so many things we consume daily. Eliminating gluten from your life isn't a matter of simply avoiding the flour and grain aisle at the grocery store. It's much more complex than that.

The first obstacle is the fact that gluten is hidden in so many foods you would never expect it to be in. When you toss your salad with a little dressing or sprinkle a bit of soy sauce into your stir fry, you're not thinking that you could be dealing with the effects of gluten shortly after you eat them. Many processed food manufacturers use gluten-containing ingredients to enhance texture, taste, and stability.

Even once you manage to eliminate gluten from your diet, there is the risk of exposure and reaction from non-dietary sources. Medications, vitamins, supplements, cosmetics, and body care products may contain gluten. The amount may be minimal, and the risk of consumption through cosmetics and body care products may be small but to the person that is severely intolerant, even a small amount of exposure can result in an undesirable reaction.

Knowledge is always power. Recognizing the main sources of gluten in your life, from both edible and non-consumable goods, enables you to take control over your health by giving you the power to choose if, when, and how much gluten you're exposed to. For people with serious gluten disease, this is a major step in regaining a sense of normalcy and control over their lives.

In this section, we're going to discuss in greater detail the sources of gluten, including foods and non-edible sources. The goal here is to provide you with a solid foundational understanding of where gluten comes from, how to avoid it, and also to understand how gluten intolerance can actually cause sensitivity to the proteins in non-gluten foods.

FOODS CONTAINING GLUTEN

Ah, food. It's something so many of us have a complicated relationship with. This relationship becomes even more complex when the foods we eat can cause immediate physical pain and/or discomfort. The standard American diet is full of foods that are far from healthy, but it often takes years for the cumulative effects of this type of diet to take hold. This isn't the case with gluten.

Individuals who are sensitive or intolerant of gluten don't need to wait years, even decades, to see and feel the effects. In the most sensitive of individuals, the effects are almost instantaneous.

Once you understand that gluten is found in certain grains, some sources of dietary gluten become obvious. We're going to go through all the grains that contain gluten, so you always have this to use as a reference point.

What becomes more troublesome when you want or need to avoid gluten is all the places gluten lurks that you would never suspect. We're also going to discuss the sneaky types of hidden gluten, and the types of foods you'll want to avoid.

I know this can all sound a bit overwhelming, especially at first as you're discovering all of the places that gluten hides. Trust me when I say that gluten-free eating becomes easier and more intuitive with experience.

Primary Sources of Dietary Gluten

Grain products are the primary sources of gluten in the average person's diet. The following grains all contain gluten, although depending on the degree of your sensitivity, you may be able to tolerate some better than others. People with Celiac disease should steer clear of all the grains on this list.

You'll notice that oats aren't included on this list. Oats are gluten-free but some people with Celiac disease or severe sensitivity can't eat them. This isn't because some oats contain gluten and others don't. The reason oats can sometimes be a problem is cross-contamination. Many times, oats are processed in facilities that process other types of grains. Therefore, oats can technically be labeled as gluten-free but may occasionally cause issues in some people.

Now for the list of grains that contain gluten.

- Wheat in all its varieties - wheat bran, wheat germ, wheat berries, etc.
- Rye, and rye flour - may sometimes be labeled as pumpernickel flour
- Barley, including flour, malt, or any other ingredient that contains the word barley
- Triticale
- Spelt
- Semolina
- Durum
- Kamut
- Bulger
- Couscous

- Farina
- Farro
- Einkorn
- Brewer's yeast
- Wheat starch
- Malt, unless made from a non-gluten source
- Specialty flours that are not labeled as gluten-free - bread flour, cake flour, etc.

If you're looking for a gluten-free flour alternative, look at options such as rice flour, almond flour, chickpea flour, cornflour, coconut flour, etc. Just make a point of checking the label for additives that may contain gluten.

Considering the list above, we can see how many types of baked goods, desserts, and processed foods contain gluten. Here is a list of common gluten-containing types of food.

- Bread, except for those made specifically with gluten-free grains
- Baked goods, including most pastries, cookies, cakes, doughnuts, and savory baked goods
- Pancakes or waffles
- Snack foods, like crackers and pretzels
- Breakfast cereals, including both hot and cold with the exception of pure oats processed in a cross contamination-free facility
- Pasta made from gluten-containing grains

- Pasta "type" foods like gnocchi and other doughs that may use grain flour as a binding agent
- Dumplings, fresh or from a mix
- Cream-based foods, like sauces, soups, or gravies that may be thickened using flour
- Anything that is made using flour or could have flour added as a binding agent.

SNEAKIER SOURCES OF DIETARY GLUTEN

The typical western diet can be a real problem for those wanting or needing to avoid gluten. If you're able to eat a diet packed with whole foods, healthy meals that you prepare yourself, and limited processed foods, you have a great deal of control over the potential for sneaky glutens to make their way into your body. Unfortunately, steering away from the typical western diet is something many people have difficulty with, due to a range of reasons from living in food deserts where lack of fresh foods is a serious issue to never having the opportunity to learn about the effects of diet on our health.

Either way, sneaky glutens are a huge issue. Food manufacturers use many types of ingredients to provide us with the texture, taste, and mouthfeel we're after, all while making their products shelf-stable to last for months on the grocery store shelves.

When you're first starting out as gluten-free, you really want to stop and look at all the labels of any processed food you pick up, unless you know for certain that it doesn't contain gluten. Honestly, you're going to find that gluten is found in foods that it seems to have no place in, and you're going to stand there in the aisle, scratching your head, thinking it's time to reconsider your overall views on the processed food industry.

The list I'm going to provide here is somewhat extensive, but it certainly isn't exhaustive. Use this list as a foundation and reference point when making your grocery list, meal planning, and finding ways to adapt your favorite foods to your new gluten-free lifestyle.

- Canned soups - gluten can be added as a thickener in cream soups or in noodles, dumplings, etc.
- Bouillons and broths
- Gravy, both jarred/canned and powdered mixes
- Rice and pasta mixes
- Condiments, including mayonnaise, salad dressings, ketchup, and premade marinades
- Soy sauce
- Teriyaki sauce
- Barbeque sauce
- Malt vinegar
- Spice blends
- Some canned foods, especially those with sauces like canned baked beans
- Processed luncheon meats
- Sausage

- Bacon
- Hot dogs
- Imitation seafood
- Meatballs, meatloaf, frozen burgers (both meat and non-meat) that use gluten ingredients to help bind the meet and provide texture
- Self-basting poultry
- Flavored meats
- Egg substitutes
- Seitan
- Flavored tofu
- Some cheeses - moldy cheeses, such as blue cheese may have been started with a wheat-based mold. Some spreadable soft cheeses, like cream cheese, may contain gluten, so always check the labels
- Non-dairy creamer
- Some flavored coffee creamers
- Puddings
- Canned fruit fillings
- Cheesecake fillings
- Pre-made pie crusts
- Frozen French fries, and some other frozen potato products that may be dusted with flour to add texture and prevent sticking during freezing
- Any food that is breaded or battered
- Frozen vegetables that come with sauce
- Some ice creams

- Hot and cold breakfast cereals
- Cereal bars
- Snack bars
- Granola
- Breakfast pastries
- Trail mix
- Nuts, with the exception of raw nuts
- Potato chips, especially those with added flavorings.

Ingredients that are Code Words for Gluten

If only avoiding gluten was as simple as looking for words like wheat, barley, rye, etc., on your food labels. Most of us have picked up a package, looked at the label, and found a list of ingredients we couldn't identify or even pronounce. Many of these ingredients are harmless and are nothing more than scientific names for common things. For example, ascorbic acid on your ingredient list, while caustic sounding, is simply added vitamin C.

Unless you're a food scientist, or chemist, deciphering all these long names on your ingredient list is challenging. Some are harmless, some are useless additives, and some can be harmful to your health, especially if you're eating gluten-free.

I want to supply you with a list of ingredients to watch out for. Again, this list isn't exhaustive, but it does contain many ingredients that are essentially scientific code words for gluten.

- Caramel coloring - this is often sourced from barley
- Yeast extract
- Brewer's yeast
- Secale cereale - another term for rye
- Natural flavorings - may be sourced from gluten-containing grains
- Artificial coloring
- Emulsifiers
- Brown rice syrup - usually contains barley-based caramel coloring
- Rice malt
- White vinegar
- White grain vinegar
- Dextrin - sometimes made from wheat (and most foods that contain dextrin from wheat will label it as so)
- Maltodextrin - the word malt typically indicates that barley was used.
- Mustard powder
- MSG
- Fermented grain extract
- Tocopherol - sometimes just listed as vitamin E
- Amino peptide complex
- Xanthan gum - sometimes derived from wheat sources
- Beta-glucan - sourced from oats, so some may be able to tolerate this
- Hordeum - followed by vulgare or distichon

- Triticum - followed by vulgare or aestivum
- Whey protein concentrate
- Hydrolyzed malt extract
- Hydrolyzed vegetable protein
- Hydrolyzed plant protein
- Hydrolyzed soy protein
- Hydrolysate
- Modified food starch
- Pregelatinized starch
- Avina sativa
- Phytosphingosine extract

Beverages Containing Gluten

While gluten is less common in beverages than other food sources, it's also more dangerous because you aren't expecting it to be there.

Many drinks that contain gluten fall into the adult category, like beer due to the hops. Still, you can't assume that all other beverages are safe for a gluten-free diet.

When you're thinking about gluten-free beverages, the more natural the better. Water, plain coffee, plain tea (including most herbal varieties), and milk are fine. Most juices are also gluten-free but be watchful if purchasing bargain brands because they sometimes include extra additives that aren't friendly for the gluten-free diet. This seems to be more of an issue with bargain apple juice.

Contrary to what one might think, wheatgrass juice is gluten-free. Wheatgrass is just the sprouted leaves of the wheat plant and doesn't contain any gluten. A word of caution here is that wheatgrass powder may contain gluten additives, so always read your labels. Also, there have been reports of wheatgrass manufacturers who claim that small amounts of gluten do show up in random samples. This is likely due to cross-contamination in the production facility.

If you're a fan of hot chocolate, you can avoid gluten by purchasing pure cocoa powder, then adding the milk, sugar, vanilla, and all the other good stuff that goes into a perfect cup of cocoa. Commercial powdered brands aren't hit or miss with gluten, so if you go that route, read your label carefully. Marshmallows in your cocoa are also okay, as long as they're made with corn starch rather than wheat starch.

One sweet beverage treat that is definitely not gluten-friendly is malted anything. You can purchase malted powder to add to milkshakes and dessert, and you might also find malted drink mixes. These are based on barley malt, so they need to be avoided. Also, skip any sweet malted drinks when eating out.

On the topic of malt, let's talk about malt liquors and alcohol that is distilled from gluten-containing grains like wheat, barley, and rye. Beer is generally produced from a combination of hops and malted barley - two things you want to avoid if living gluten-free. There are a growing number of gluten-free beers on the market to try.

Concerning hard spirits distilled from gluten-containing grains, the advice is a little murkier. In theory, the distillation process removes gluten from the alcohol. Gluten is a protein and can't be broken down by distillation. Therefore, it shouldn't make its way to the final product. On the opposite side are those who are sensitive to gluten, claiming that all types of whiskey (bourbon, rye, scotch, etc.) leave them with gluten-related symptoms. Some individuals also have issues with vodka that use wheat or rye in the distillation process.

If you are sensitive to gluten-grain based alcohols, you can happily make your cocktails with spirits that aren't distilled using gluten grains. Tequila, rum, gins, and many types of cordials are distilled from non-gluten ingredients. Use caution when ordering mixed cocktails or adding mixers to your drinks because those may contain gluten.

Generally speaking, all types of wines should be safe for a gluten-free diet. The only exception might be specialty wines that have a barley-based caramel color added to them.

The bottom line here is to keep your beverages as simplistic as possible and know what you're drinking. Plain coffee is gluten-free but that bottled coffee concoction from the check-out lane refrigerator might not be. A latte from your favorite coffee house is likely fine but their coffee "freezes" made with a special mix might pose a problem. If in doubt ask, and always read your labels.

NON-FOOD PRODUCTS CONTAINING GLUTEN

One of the most challenging aspects of living a gluten-free life is the realization that gluten is in places that you would have never imagined. Gluten isn't just found in food and beverages but also in products that you use every day. If you're simply trying to avoid gluten to improve your health, you may be able to tolerate these sneaky sources of gluten. For those with Celiac disease, even the slightest exposure can be devastating and dangerous.

We've taken some time to discuss the food and beverage sources of gluten. Now, I'd like to talk to you about the hidden sources of gluten in non-food items that you need to be aware of.

Does Gluten Really Matter If You Aren't Consuming It?

This is a question I often hear, and it's an important one. There's certainly an argument that gluten's risk is minimal at best if you aren't actually consuming it. What this argument doesn't take into consideration are all the ways that gluten from non-food items can still make their way into the body. This is especially important for people with Celiac disease.

Let's take for example, lipsticks and lip glosses or balms. These products often contain a type of gluten. You probably haven't tried eating Chapstick since you were a child but there is still a risk of consumption each time you slather it on. These products can easily find their way into your mouth, be transferred via food, or be absorbed through a tiny cut or cold sore. Your body doesn't care how the gluten got there; it's still going to react.

Whether you personally need to watch out for gluten in non-food items is really a matter of how sensitive you are to gluten and the severity of your symptoms. If you haven't experienced any notable symptoms of sensitivity to gluten, then checking the labels of all the products I'm about to mention (and more) might not be worth your time. If you have Celiac disease or are extremely sensitive, it becomes important to research, read labels, and avoid any and all gluten-containing products.

We're going to start by going over the main non-food sources of gluten, and then follow up with a list of other items/products to keep a close eye on if you have gluten sensitivity or intolerance.

Medications

This, in my opinion, is one of the most dangerous sources of hidden gluten. If you have a doctor you've been working with who is aware of your issues with gluten, they can help you avoid accidentally exposing yourself through medications. What is more troublesome is the number of people with undiagnosed or misdiagnosed gluten issues that take these medications every day.

As of last year, a bill was introduced to congress called the Gluten in Medicine Disclosure Act of 2019. Currently, the bill has been referred to the Senate Subcommittee on Health, but no official action has been taken beyond that. The goal of the bill was to require disclosure of gluten-containing ingredients in medications.

Gluten-containing ingredients aren't used in medications for their therapeutic purposes but instead for their binding properties. Different types of binders are used in medications. It's important to note that a brand name and generic form of medication may use different types of binders, meaning that one may contain gluten while the other doesn't.

Fortunately, there aren't many medications that use these types of binders but it's up to you to know which ingredients pose a risk, ask your doctor or pharmacist questions about the presence of these ingredients, and read labels to protect your health.

The following ingredients are considered red flags for those with gluten sensitivity or intolerance.

- Wheat
- Starch - modified starch, pregelatinized starch, pregelatinized modified starch (more specifically when the source of the starch isn't specified)
- Dextrin, unless it is sourced from corn or potato
- Dextrimaltose sourced from barley malt
- Dextrates, with unknown source origin
- Caramel coloring, if sourced from barley malt.

Vitamins and Supplements

I'm not going to dwell on this category too much because much of what we discussed about gluten in medications apply here. Gluten is sometimes used as a binding agent in some vitamins and supplements. Although it isn't common, it's important to be aware of the potential.

One additional issue that exists for vitamins and supplements is the risk of cross-contamination. Even if a product doesn't contain gluten specifically, the production of grain-based fillers and artificial colors or flavorings presents a cross-contamination risk.

Cosmetics and Beauty Products

Cosmetics and beauty products are an often overlooked source of gluten. This might not seem like a big deal on the surface, after all, how often are you consuming your cosmetics and beauty products? The problem is that these types of products may be consumed via transfer, without even thinking about it. Skincare products and cosmetics may contain ingredients like wheat germ oil, or other types of wheat, barley, etc., derived ingredients.

Of course, the main issue is that these products will find their way to a person's mouth and that they can be transferred by licking one's lips, from fingers, or even from drinking glasses or utensils. A bath product containing gluten might accidentally get splashed onto the face. Another viable way to consider is that our bodies are covered with pores and we absorb anything that is put onto the skin. The possibilities of gluten transfer in this case are many.

Preliminary research tells us that the quantity of gluten that may be transferred from cosmetics and beauty products is negligible but doesn't discount it entirely. There also exists the possibility of gluten-related skin irritation, especially in people with Celiac disease.

Some cosmetics and beauty products are labeled gluten-free, but these are few and far between. If you're someone with a serious sensitivity of intolerance to gluten, I strongly urge you to familiarize yourself with the most common gluten ingredients in these types of products. The following list, while not exhaustive, is a good reference point for the most common gluten additives you'll find in health and beauty products.

- Wheat, Triticum, or gluten: Look or ingredients such as hydrolyzed wheat protein, hydrolyzed wheat gluten, Triticum lipids (or any ingredient that features Triticum), wheat bran extract, wheat germ extract.
- Barley, malt, or Hordeum vulgare: Any ingredient with one of these names, including extracts.
- Rye or Secale
- Oats (due to the potential for cross-contamination).

Play-Doh

Play-Doh, along with off brands of this moldable clay-like substance that seems to be a staple of nearly everyone's childhood contains gluten. Play-Doh may be considered non-toxic, but it isn't without its dangers for gluten sensitive or intolerant children.

Children are notorious for putting everything in their mouths and touching just about everything they can. This is part of their wonderful curiosity that helps them learn more about the world around them. Even if the child doesn't put the Play-Doh in their mouth, the stuff gets under fingernails and seems to get stuck there for days, even with a good, long soak in the tub.

This is a problem not only for children with gluten issues but for adults too. The gluten from the dough may transfer to the table where meals are consumed, to shared touched surfaces, or even by giving hugs or holding hands.

Avoiding gluten doesn't mean you or your child need to miss out on the experience of squeezing and squishing colorful dough into all sorts of creations though. Homemade craft doughs made with gluten-free flour work just as well. Plus, you can color them or even add natural scents (like lavender or chamomile to play with before bedtime).

Other Potential Non-Food Sources of Gluten Exposure

- Hair care products: Shampoo, conditioners, hairspray
- Dental care products: toothpaste, mouthwash, dental plastics or sealants
- Sunscreens and lotions
- Laundry detergent
- Body wash or soap
- Adhesives on envelopes and stamps.

Additional ingredients to look out for:

- Barley, in any form including extracts and lipids (may be labeled as Hordeum distichon or Hordeum vulgare
- Barley-based amino-peptide complex
- Beta-glucan, which comes from oats but carries a cross-contamination risk
- Dextrin
- Hydrolyzed wheat protein, sometimes labeled as wheat hydrolysate, wheat peptides, or simply HWP
- Fermented yeast, also listed as phytosphingosine extract
- Starch/pregelatinized starch
- Triticum
- Wheat germ
- Yeast Extract
- Xanthan gum (sometimes sourced from wheat).

The Lesser-Known Challenges of Living Gluten-Free

By far, aside from health issues, one of the most challenging aspects of living gluten-free is learning to identify the gluten in your life and eliminating it. This is made even more difficult by convoluted labeling and less than ideal food packaging regulations.

I truly cannot stress enough the importance of learning to read food labels and being able to identify sources of gluten on your own. The list supplied above is a good start, and as time-consuming as it might seem, checking each label truly is important for your health.

Some food manufacturers try to help you identify gluten-free foods with special labeling. I want to urge you not to trust this labeling alone, and to still look at the list of ingredients if a food claims to be gluten-free.

The reason for this is that the term gluten-free isn't as all-encompassing as you might think. According to the FDA, food can contain up to 20ppm (parts per million) and be considered safe for Celiac disease, and thus be approved as gluten-free food. Is the 20ppm an incredibly low amount? Yes, but extremely sensitive individuals might still react, even at these low levels. The average person who has gluten sensitivity may have no issue but for those with a more serious disease, this might not be the case.

There's another term I want to bring up here, and that's "wheat-free". In our minds, we make a natural association between wheat and gluten, thinking if something is wheat-free that it must also be gluten-free. A look at the above list of gluten-containing foods tells us otherwise. Wheat-free foods are designated as such for individuals who have an allergy/sensitivity to wheat itself, and not necessarily gluten across the board - although the two can go hand in hand.

Food packaging also contains allergen information. You'll find keywords like wheat, soy, dairy, eggs, etc. found there. If you see a product that contains wheat, that makes it a given for also containing gluten. However, if nothing is listed in the allergen information, this doesn't mean that it's free from gluten. Gluten isn't considered an allergen and won't be listed on its own here. Always, always check the ingredient label to make sure.

Cross-Reactivity and Why It's Dangerous

If you manage to eliminate all gluten from your diet, you should be free and clear from suffering all the ill effects of gluten on your health, or so it would seem. For people with gluten sensitivity, and especially gluten intolerance, this isn't always the case.

Most people who are either sensitive or intolerant of gluten, including those that have been diagnosed with Celiac disease, have a variant of the Human Leukocyte Antigen (HLA) gene. Two variants are found - DQ2 and DQ8. These gene variants affect how the body recognizes and responds to gluten. These variants are quite common, affecting a little over half of the general population, which is enough to argue that most people could do well with eliminating or at least reducing the gluten in their diet but that isn't the point of this section.

What we do need to talk about is how these mutations cause your body to produce antibodies against gluten, which we've established is a protein. The problem is that these antibodies will sometimes react to proteins in other types of foods, ones that don't contain gluten, yet react as if they have encountered gluten. This is called gluten cross-reactivity.

There is a list of foods where this molecular mimicry, where a type of protein from one food is molecularly similar to the gluten protein, occurs. Not every person with gluten sensitivity or intolerance will have a cross-reaction to every one of these foods. Still, it is important to understand the physiological mechanisms at work here. So many people work hard to eliminate gluten from their lives, yet still experience symptoms of gluten-intolerance, which for some can be debilitating.

The list of foods that can cause gluten cross-reactions, include both foods you might expect, like other types of grains, and those that wouldn't even make it onto your radar as possible irritants. Foods that present a risk of gluten cross-reaction includes:

- Rice

- Corn
- Potato
- Amaranth
- Quinoa
- Hemp
- Millet
- Buckwheat
- Sorghum
- Teff
- Coffee
- Soy
- Dairy
- Chocolate
- Yeast
- Tapioca
- Yeast
- Eggs

CHAPTER SUMMARY

In this chapter, we have discussed the primary sources of gluten exposure, including both food and non-edible products. We've learned key identifying ingredients that indicate whether a product contains gluten, as well as recognizing how gluten is hidden in many of the foods we eat. Specifically, we have discussed:

- Gluten is a protein found in wheat, barley, rye, and other grains;
- Ingredients that contain gluten are often added to processed foods to enhance taste, texture, and product stability;
- Gluten is found in many foods you'd never expect it to be in, from frozen French fries to ketchup;
- Some beverages contain gluten, especially those that are flavored or powdered;
- Non-food sources of exposure include medications, supplements, health and beauty products, and some children's' products;
- People with gluten sensitivity or intolerance have gene variants that affect how their bodies react to gluten proteins;
- Through molecular mimicry, your body may recognize non-gluten proteins as gluten and produce an adverse reaction. This is called cross-reactivity.

In the next chapter, we're going to discuss how to successfully adopt a gluten-free diet and enjoy improved health as a result.

5

THE GLUTEN-FREE DIET - A ROAD TO HEALTH

Here is the question I know that many of you are asking - "What Exactly Can You Eat on a Gluten-Free Diet?".

The entirety of the last chapter was devoted to helping you identify the many sources of gluten in your diet. This included information on all the hidden sources of gluten, which I know can be overwhelming, especially if you're just starting on this way of eating. You might even feel like everything about your old way of eating needs to be tossed out the window, and that you're just not sure how you can adjust and make all these changes. If you live with others and share your meals with them, this process of switching over to a completely gluten-free diet is even more challenging.

I think a problem that occurs almost every time when someone embarks on a healthier way of eating is that they feel deprived in some ways. This is completely normal, and these feelings can exist, even when you know the changes you're making are necessary for your health. These feelings can be even more substantial when you feel that you don't have a choice.

In this chapter, we're going to help you shift toward a more positive mindset regarding all these changes and focus on what you can have. This includes learning how to adapt some of your favorite gluten-containing foods so that you can continue to enjoy them.

My goal in this chapter is to help you see the freedom that comes with eating gluten-free. Freedom from pain, discomfort, and poor health. The freedom of worrying that every bite of food comes with undesirable consequences. The freedom of feeling restricted by the gluten-containing, processed food that lines supermarket shelves. Freedom from all of this and so much more.

Contrary to how it may seem, living gluten-free doesn't equate to dietary deprivation. To illustrate this point, let's begin by supplying a list of completely gluten-free foods.

Gluten-Free Grains

Living gluten-free doesn't mean you have to give up grains entirely. I strongly encourage you to include gluten-free grains in your diet. Grains contain vitamins, trace minerals, and lots of good fiber that your body needs.

The grains on this list are gluten-free and make for easy and delicious substitutes for the gluten-containing grains you may be accustomed to eating. Some will sound familiar to you and be easy substitutions in your diet. Others might require a bit of a learning curve when it comes to preparation and adapting your tastes.

I do have a few words of caution when using the substitute grains on this list. In the previous chapter, we briefly discussed the risk of cross-contamination in facilities where both gluten-free and gluten-containing grains are processed. The risk may be small, and the grains may be contaminated and still fall below the FDA's 20ppm guidelines for gluten-free foods. The average person is likely to be affected by the small amount of gluten that may be present in these foods. If you have severe gluten disease, it is important to at least be aware of the risk and monitor yourself for any symptoms.

The second issue, which we also discussed in the previous chapter is cross-reactivity, where your body mistakes other types of proteins for gluten and responds accordingly. I suggest keeping a detailed food diary for at least a few weeks, if not a month or two, to help you recognize any potential cross-reaction issues that may exist.

Now, with that out of the way, let's talk about all the delicious grains you can enjoy on a gluten-free diet.

Rice - brown rice, wild rice, white rice, short grain,

long grain...practically any of the many types of rice from around the world. Stay away from rice/grain blends that may include gluten-containing grains. Also, avoid flavored rice mixes that contain powdered flavor and spice mixes.

Quinoa- This mild, neutral grain is gluten-free and has gained popularity in recent years. Quinoa was mentioned in the previous chapter because of the risk of cross-contamination and cross-reactivity. Again, this grain is generally considered safe for those with gluten-sensitivity or gluten-intolerance but it's a smart idea to monitor yourself for symptoms and stick with a brand that you know and trust.

Amaranth - This versatile, gluten-free grain has been cultivated for thousands of years. It is nutritionally dense and has a texture that's a bit chewier and "meatier" than rice. Some people like to "pop" amaranth kernels in a skillet for a snack that's similar to popcorn but more nutritionally rich. Like Quinoa, there may be a cross-reaction risk with amaranth, so monitor your reaction the first few times you consume this grain.

Buckwheat - Don't let the "wheat" in buckwheat throw you off from this gluten-free grain. Buckwheat has nearly four times the fiber of regular wheat and its flour is a great substitute for wheat flour in pancakes, muffins, and other baked goods. Buckwheat groats, especially with some fruit and a little spice, make for a hearty, filling, hot breakfast on cold mornings.

Millet - This is a small, almost pearl-like whole grain. As a grain, millet is resistant, being able to withstand less than desirable growing conditions. Millet is rich in essential amino acids, which are a building block of protein, making this gluten-free grain an excellent, natural source of dietary protein. It's also high in fiber, magnesium, and folate. You can cook millet and eat it as a whole grain, although soaking before cooking is recommended. You can also purchase millet flour to use as a substitute for wheat flour in your recipes.

Sorghum - Due to its high antioxidant content, sorghum is considered a gluten-free, super-grain. Sorghum is more widely known in the south than in the north, but it is quickly becoming a staple in gluten-free households. The whole grain is easy to cook and versatile. Sorghum flour is also available, making for an easy substitute for wheat flour with few adaptations needed.

Teff - This gluten-free grain is a type of seed. Teff is considered one of the smallest grains in the world. Running a handful of this tiny grain through your fingers may remind you more of spices rather than a typical grain. Teff can be a little more expensive than other types of gluten-free grains, which can make it a little cost-prohibitive if you're on a strict grocery budget. Due to its small size, teff is easy to cook and makes a nice alternative for pilaf style dishes or as a gluten-free stuffing.

Tapioca - Many people don't recognize tapioca beyond its role in an old-fashioned dessert called tapioca pudding. Tapioca has many culinary uses and is often found as an additive in foods because it can work as both a thickener and emulsifier. Tapioca comes from the cassava root and holds little nutritional value. It's almost purely starch, which means it shouldn't be the star of the show at dinnertime (which is good because it wouldn't hold up that well anyway). Still, tapioca is a good option to add to desserts or its flour can be used as a thickening agent in place of wheat flour.

Arrowroot - Arrowroot is commonly sold as a powder in the baking aisle. The powder is white and soft, similar to cornstarch or powdered sugar. It is mild flavored and is perfect for blending into gravies, sauces, or for thickening soups. If you like to coat ingredients with a little flour when cooking, such as with stew, arrowroot makes an excellent substitute for wheat flour.

Oats - Oats are technically gluten-free. Of all the gluten-free grains, oats probably have the biggest risk of gluten cross-contamination. This mostly because of the scale that oats are processed and sold in stores. If you do choose to consume oats, stay away from instant oatmeal products that are flavored. The flavoring mixes are almost a guarantee to contain some form of gluten.

STAPLES OF YOUR GLUTEN-FREE DIET

Once we move outside of grains and processed foods, you'll find that there is a bounty of gluten-free foods to include in your diet every day. In this section, I want to provide you with a list of gluten-free staples that you can plan your meals and snacks around. Occasionally, there might be exceptions to the foods I list here. In those cases, I will make a note so that you know what to look for to ensure you're choosing a truly gluten-free food.

Fruits and Vegetables

The produce section of your grocery store is packed with fresh fruits and vegetables that are naturally gluten-free. The list here is just a sample of what you might find in your local produce section, so don't be afraid to venture outside of what you see here and experiment with different fruits and vegetables to add some variety to your diet.

Fresh is always better if you have access to it and the ability to restock as needed. If you choose canned fruits or vegetables, check labels to make sure they don't contain added flavorings, spices, or sauces that contain gluten. You should also always check the labels on pre-chopped, dried, or frozen fruits and vegetables just to ensure no gluten was added during preparation or packaging.

- Apples

- Bananas
- Oranges
- Grapefruit
- Lime
- Lemon
- Tangerines
- Peaches
- Nectarines
- Pears
- Pineapple
- Mango
- Coconut
- Watermelon, and other types of melon
- Berries
- Kiwi
- Papaya
- Broccoli
- Cauliflower
- Potatoes
- Corn
- Squash
- Spinach
- Kale
- Salad greens
- Bell peppers
- Sweet potatoes
- Mushrooms

- Onion
- Radishes
- Brussel sprouts
- Turnips
- Beets
- Artichoke
- Cabbage
- Eggplant
- Garlic
- Scallion
- Zucchini

Meats and Protein

Generally speaking, the meats you find at your local butcher or the meat department of your grocery store are gluten-free - as long as they are just cuts of meat without any additives. Gluten becomes an issue when meats are breaded, battered, or are coated, or injected with flavorings and spice mixes.

Many processed types of meat also contain gluten. If you have a craving for lunch meat or sausage, you'll want to search out specifically gluten-free brands.

Except for tofu, processed plant-based proteins can also present an issue for the gluten-free person. Veggie burgers or processed plant-based protein products often contain gluten ingredients that are used for binding and texture. There are, of course, exceptions. A good rule of thumb is to assume these foods contain gluten, and then be presently surprised when you happen to come across one that is truly gluten-free.

You'll also find beans and legumes on this list. Dry beans and legumes are best. Stay away from packages of dry beans that are mixed with spices and intended to be used as soup bases. Most plain, canned beans are fine but check the labels just in case. Beans with seasonings and sauces, such as canned baked beans, are often sneaky sources of beans containing gluten.

- Beef
- Chicken
- Pork
- Turkey
- Duck
- Lamb
- Fish
- Shellfish
- Unflavored tofu
- Tempeh
- Beans - chickpeas, lentils, peas, kidney beans, pinto beans, black beans, white beans, black-eyed peas
- Nuts - all nuts are gluten-free in their raw form. Gluten may be added when nuts are roasted or seasoned

Dairy

Most dairy products are naturally gluten-free. Gluten becomes an issue when flavorings are added, as is the case with chocolate milk or flavored cream cheese. Extremely gluten-sensitive individuals may experience symptoms when they consume moldy cheeses that have included some type of wheat product to initiate mold production. This isn't an issue for many but it's something you should be aware of.

- Milk, non-flavored
- Plant-based milk, non-flavored, check ingredients
- Butter
- Ghee
- Cheese, natural, unflavored
- Cream cheese - check labels
- Heavy Cream, whipping cream
- Cottage cheese
- Sour cream
- Plain yogurt

Baking, Condiments, and Extras

Living gluten-free doesn't mean going without all of your favorite homemade favorites or eating only bland foods. Keep this list of gluten-free staples in your pantry.

- Vegetable oils

- Coconut oil
- Olive oil
- Sesame oil
- Cooking sprays - double-check the label
- Honey
- Jams and jellies
- Sugars - white, brown, confectioners
- Pure maple syrup
- Corn syrup (avoid any brand that uses caramel coloring)
- Apple cider vinegar
- Distilled vinegar
- White vinegar
- Salt
- Pepper
- Individual spices that aren't part of a blend

I want to stress again that these lists of gluten-free foods are not exhaustive. It would be impossible to list every gluten-free food on the shelves of your local grocery store, convenience store, or farmer's market. As a general rule of thumb, the fresher the better. So much of the gluten we consume today comes from additives like flavorings and texturizers. This isn't to say that all natural foods are gluten-free but you're definitely improving your odds of not consuming hidden glutens when you start with foods that are as simple and basic as possible.

Living Gluten-Free Doesn't Mean Giving Up All Your Favorites

Nobody likes to feel deprived of the things they love, and when it comes to food, we can form very strong emotional attachments to certain dishes. There has been some interesting research into the foods we crave depending upon our moods. When we're sad, we're more likely to reach for comforting but sweet foods like ice cream, cakes, or cookies. What's interesting is that sweet cravings are also associated with joy and contentment, possibly because we associate sweet treats with happy occasions and celebrations.

We crave salt when we're bored, something crunchy when we're irritated or angry, and spicy foods are associated with excitement or times of increased energy. We're all human and experience a range of these emotions, which means we're also going to experience a range of cravings to go along with it.

Many of us also build memories and traditions around food. Sitting around the table and talking while enjoying a meal is a way of connection. Almost every holiday celebration involves a meal as the centerpiece of the celebration. Unless you've been living gluten-free for years, these occasions probably haven't included a long list of gluten-free favorites.

There is also the challenge of eating gluten-free when others in your home don't want to. Whether you're choosing this lifestyle because you want to or because you need to for health reasons, you have the right to make dietary choices that support your health. Unfortunately, it isn't always easy to get others on board with these changes. At best, you might get some resistance to change. At the worst, you might receive downright refusal to play along with the changes.

One of the things I always want to tell my clients when they are thinking about going gluten-free is that they don't have to give up their favorites. You can still have your holiday favorites, your weeknight staples, your favorite snacks, and the little things you indulge in when your moods are feeling a certain way.

There are so many great alternatives to gluten ingredients that with a little food knowledge and some experimentation in the kitchen, you can recreate almost all of your gluten-containing favorites - and often you and everyone else won't be able to tell the difference.

In the remainder of this chapter, we're going to talk about the best gluten-free substitutions for baking, cooking, and preparing your favorite foods. We're also going to go over a few of the tried and true tricks for substituting gluten-free ingredients while not sacrificing quality or flavor.

Gluten-Free Substitutions for Baking

<u>Alternatives for wheat flours</u> - coconut flour, chickpea flour, almond flour, quinoa flour, amaranth flour, hemp flour, coconut flour, banana flour, tapioca flour, chestnut flour, cornstarch.

Alternatives for pie or cookie bar crusts - gluten-free cookies or gluten-free nuts, crushed or chopped and mixed with butter or coconut oil.

Breadings - gluten-free flours, which you can season yourself, gluten-free baking mixes, cornmeal, cornflour, crushed potato chips (check ingredients if flavored).

Thickeners and emulsifiers - cornstarch, arrowroot, tapioca.

Breadcrumbs and croutons - dried or toasted gluten-free bread.

Tips for Substituting with Gluten-Free Ingredients

Learning how to cook or bake using new ingredients can feel like an intimidating process. Change, while often a positive thing, is rarely easy. You have your favorites that you've been making the same way for years. Or, maybe you're not one to spend much time in the kitchen at all, and going gluten-free means you'll need to try your hand at developing at least some basic culinary skills since gluten seems to be everywhere in prepackaged or take-out food.

Wherever you're coming from, I truly do want to urge you to see this as an adventure in improving your health. You're going to learn a lot of new things along the way, discovering how to cook new dishes or recreate your tried and true favorites, being among them. This process can be fun as long as you see it that way. Exploring new things like a kid exploring the next fun adventure.

So far in this section, we've talked about gluten-free alternatives to common foods. It's great to have this information but only goes so far if you're not sure what to do with it. Now, we're going to change direction a little and talk about how to best put all these gluten-free substitutions to use in your daily life.

Baking with new ingredients is an area of concern that I see with my clients. Creating the perfect texture or consistency with baked goods can be challenging enough. Add in flours, thickeners, and emulsifiers that act differently, and you can expect a little trial and error. Fortunately for you, and all of us really, the gluten-free "trend" is nothing new. For some time now, creative culinary types have experimented, explored, and documented their gluten-free success and failures. For you and me, this means there are almost endless resources out there for gluten-free cooking tips, recipes, and how to adopt a gluten-free diet into your lifestyle.

I'm going to take some of the inspiration I've found from gluten-free experts, along with my own trial and error, and use all this knowledge to provide you with some good, basic tips to get started.

Baking with Gluten-Free Ingredients

Wheat flour is what's used in most baked goods. It works as a binder, thanks to the gluten. The gluten creates this matrix which you could almost describe as glue. It's what holds baked goods together and gives them their doughy texture.

If you've ever kneaded bread or stuck your hands into any type of flour-based dough, you've felt gluten at work. Gluten is what makes the dough sticky and springy. It's difficult to recreate this with non-gluten flours but it's not impossible.

The type of baked good you want to make will determine how you go about substituting in gluten-free ingredients. If a recipe calls for just a small amount of wheat flour, chances are good that you can just do a simple substitution for the same amount of non-gluten flour. This would be the case in a recipe where a few tablespoons or ¼ cup of flour was used to bind or maybe thicken. In this type of recipe, you're not looking for the gluten protein matrix to do a lot of work, so substituting is easy.

In baked goods like bread, cakes, or cookies, you have to be more strategic in how you substitute in non-gluten flours. The first thing to consider is the type of wheat flour you'd normally use and the desired outcome.

Bread flour, which is higher in protein, develops a lot of gluten. This type of flour is preferred for bread and when you need a baked good to rise or develop a type of airy, doughy texture. On the opposite end of the spectrum is cake flour, which is lower in protein and doesn't provide the same doughy, sticky texture. Instead, it's used mostly to bind and keep everything from crumbling apart.

Non-gluten flours aren't going to recreate these results exactly because they're missing the gluten protein. However, choosing the right non-gluten flour can help you closely mimic the results. This is especially easy in baked goods that use a lower protein flour, or don't rely on good gluten formation, as is the case with pie crust.

If you're new to baking, especially if you're new to using gluten-free flours, I'd suggest that you start with baked goods that would normally use a lower protein flour or that are not dependent on the sticky gluten matrix for texture. Pie crusts, brownies, and cookies are a great place to start because flour is mostly used as a binder, so it's easier to substitute gluten-free alternatives.

Let's look at the different low protein, high protein, and starch-based non-gluten alternatives for baking.

Low Protein Non-Gluten Flour Alternatives

Substituting low protein flour in your baked goods is pretty easy. Non-gluten flours made from rice, corn, or millet are very low in protein. Most people who have had success with gluten-free baking have learned how to mix different non-gluten flours to create better texture and flavor in their baked goods. If you use just rice flour or just cornflour, your baked goods might end up being a little crumbly. Mixing one of these flours with a small amount of higher protein non-gluten flour will help solve this issue.

Rice flour has a mild taste that works well with many types of baked goods. The one problem with it is that it can become a bit gummy once it's mixed in with wet ingredients. Again, mixing in a bit of another type of non-gluten flour can mostly solve this issue.

Corn flour has a soft texture that blends well but it also has a stronger taste. This flour might be good to use in baked goods that have flavors that would go well with corn. Think along the lines of cinnamon, nutmeg, apples, carrot cake, etc. Also, note that cornflour and cornmeal are two completely different things. You can't substitute one for the other.

Millet flour is a little harder to find. You might have to visit a health or natural foods store that has a decent gluten-free baking section. Millet flour is also mild-flavored, and its texture is often preferred over that of rice flour.

You do have many other options for lower protein gluten-free flours, but they also come with flavor profiles that aren't always great for baking. If you use buckwheat flour, quinoa flour, or amaranth flour, expect to taste them. These grain flours would work well for savory flatbreads but wouldn't be a suitable substitution on their own in your favorite brownie recipe.

The flours mentioned above are good non-gluten substitutions when you want to make:

- Flatbreads
- Thin pizza crust

- Dense baked goods like brownies or a denser type of cake
- Pie crusts
- Mixed with a liquid for breading or battering
- Coating vegetables or meats before cooking
- Using as a thickener for gravies, sauces, soups, etc.

High Protein Non-Gluten Flour Alternatives

Unlike the low protein flour alternatives, higher protein non-gluten flours aren't made from grains. Instead, they're made from plant-based protein sources like chickpeas or soybeans. Using these types of non-gluten flour is a little tricky and may require some experimentation. Their higher protein counts make them better suited for bread, rolls, and other baked goods you want to have a denser, heartier texture.

These flours can have a taste that is strong and very reminiscent of the protein sources they come from. It's best to mix this type of flour with a milder flavored lower protein variety, just to give the final products some balance of flavor. More than one person has attempted to make bread from garbanzo flour, only to find that their finished product tasted like chewy hummus. A balance of flavors here is really important.

Starchy Non-Gluten Flour Alternatives

Starches are the simplest category of non-gluten alternatives. These flours are used for thickening or dredging and work identically to their gluten counterparts. If you want to make gravy, thicken a soup, or dust a bread pan before baking, these starches can easily be substituted for regular wheat flour.

- Cornstarch
- Arrowroot
- Potato starch
- Tapioca starch

5 Beginning Gluten-Free Baking Tips

1. Make it easy on yourself. You can purchase gluten-free flour mixes that have already been formulated for specific types of baked goods. You can buy gluten-free flour mixes for bread, cakes, cookies, etc. This can help take some of the guesswork out and give you a little more confidence as you navigate your way through the beginning stages of gluten-free living.
2. Consider the uniqueness of gluten-free flour. Gluten-free flour acts differently than wheat flour in baked goods, so plan on adjusting as you go. You'll need to add a bit more liquid sometimes, let the dough rest a little longer for it to form properly, and work quickly with it before it dries out. There's a learning curve here, so be gentle with yourself.
3. Learn from others. Ask a roomful of people to describe the perfect cookie and you're going to get a bunch of

different answers. We all like different things, so it's important to find recipes that are aligned with your preferences. Research, follow gluten-free blogs and read lots of recipes - as well as reviews. What works for one isn't going to work for everyone but if you look around, you're more likely to find recipes that you'll enjoy.

4. Choose one thing to master with gluten-free alternatives. Maybe start slow and try a low-protein gluten-free flour in your next sauce. Work at it until it's perfect for you. Maybe work on the perfect batter for onion rings or tempura. Try a dense, chewy brownie recipe that will be delicious even if you don't get the texture just right. This only makes it all the more fun to try again.

5. Used formed containers for your baked goods. Without gluten, baked goods simply don't hold their structure as well during baking. If you set a loaf of gluten-free bread dough in the middle of a sheet pan, chances are you're going to have something that more closely resembles flatbread when it comes out of the oven. Bread pans, cake pans, and muffin tins will help your baked goods hold their shape.

CHAPTER SUMMARY

In this chapter, we talked about the best gluten-free alternatives to use in cooking and baking, as well as some tips for recreating your favorites in a gluten-free kitchen. Specifically, we have discussed:

- Gluten-free grains are aplenty and found in almost every grocery store;
- Gluten-free grains are nutritious, containing high amounts of fiber, vitamins, and minerals;
- There is a range of textures and tastes in gluten-free grains;
- Gluten-free flours are made from gluten-free grains, plant-based proteins, and other foods like coconut or bananas;
- Like there are different types of wheat flours, there are also different types of non-gluten flours. Learning which ones to use in different recipes is key to success;
- With a little practice and willingness to learn, you can recreate your old favorites.

In the next chapter, we're going to take everything we've learned so far and use it to develop a strategy for developing a successful gluten-free lifestyle.

6

CREATING A GLUTEN-FREE HABIT

You have absorbed an incredible amount of information leading up to this point. You've learned a lot about gluten, the effects it can have on your health, and what it means to live gluten-free. The time has come to take everything you've learned so far and put it into action.

I say "everything that you've learned so far" because the opportunities for learning and growth on this journey are endless. Not only is there more you can learn by researching more on these topics yourself, but the medical and scientific communities are also continually providing new research and new insights.

I hope you're excited about the changes you're about to make. I also know that changes, especially eliminating gluten, can be stressful. Feeling a little stressed or overwhelmed is completely normal but there are things you can do to make the transition easier.

In this chapter, we're going to talk about how to smoothly transition into a gluten-free life, how to set yourself up for success, and how in just 60 days, this new gluten-free undertaking will be solidified as a healthy, lifelong habit.

7 TIPS FOR SIMPLIFYING YOUR TRANSITION TO GLUTEN-FREE

When I work with my clients on developing a gluten-free lifestyle, I'm always intrigued by their reactions along the way. On one hand, it's exciting and empowering to know you can take back control of your health. That if you make a few changes to how you eat, your digestive health and so many other health issues can begin to heal. The body is miraculous, and I often see in their eyes the moment my clients realize this.

Change is also difficult and overwhelming. You don't know how to successfully do something until you've actually done it. Sometimes even finding a starting point feels impossible.

It's perfectly normal to feel like you're chasing your tail a little when first starting out. As unsure of yourself that you might seem right now, in 60 days you're going to be living a different life and gaining back control of your life. All the little details that you're struggling with today will seem like second nature. As adults, we sometimes forget the process of learning something new. It takes time, and we often need more than a little guidance.

A little bit later in this chapter, we're going to talk about the 60-day, life-changing game plan to improve your health by adopting a gluten-free lifestyle. Before we get there, I want to talk about a few of my favorite tips for simplifying your transition.

1. Have a Support Network. Even before you take a bit of your first gluten-free cookie, you should have some type of support network in place. If you have support from friends or family, especially if they are also gluten-free or willing to go through this transition with you, then that is great.

The reality is that not everyone has this. Fortunately, there is no shortage of support networks that are going to welcome you with open arms. If you're someone who likes to meet with people face to face, or you're interested in making local friends that share your dietary goals check your local community calendars for gluten-free support groups. If you can't find a group, look for gluten-free cooking classes that are often offered by fitness centers, hospitals, or other health-centered organizations. You're sure to meet some like-minded people this way.

There are also plenty of online communities that you can join. I would suggest joining several and observing them for a bit until you find the ones that fit.

2. Get Out of the Poor Me Mindset Sooner, Rather Than Later. Many of us associate dietary changes with deprivation. We feel like we're being forced to give up the things we love. I want to encourage you to swap out this mindset for a more positive one. Taking back control of your health is empowering. There's nothing "poor me" about it. Improving your health will open up more opportunities than you had before. Again, no deprivation there.

If you feel like you're getting stuck on thinking of all the foods you can't have, stop and turn it around. Think of all the delicious foods you can have. Maybe you can't have a doughy piece of garlic bread with your pasta but you can have a luscious Caprese salad, a flavorful soup with wild rice, and berry compote drizzled with fresh cream for dessert. That really doesn't ring of deprivation, does it? Also, you can still find delicious gluten free garlic bread out there even if you don't make it yourself and you can still have delicious gluten free pasta that can taste just about the same and if not, better. Just use your resources and look.

3. Get Excited About Starting Fresh. One of the steps in the 60-day plan is to go through your kitchen, clean it out, replace old worn-out utensils and small appliances, and make room to experiment in the kitchen. There's just something refreshing and reviving about cleaning out the old to make room for the new. Some might think it's going a bit too far but if you have it in your budget and ability, this is a great time to freshen up the look of your kitchen, try some new colors, and go for something different. Even a new set of dishes or new canisters to hold your gluten-free grains can give you a nice mental boost.

4. Get a Slow Cooker. Speaking of updating your kitchen, if you don't have a slow cooker or pressure cooker, now is a great time to get one. These time-saving devices make it easy to throw some gluten-free ingredients together in a pot and have it ready to eat when you get home. When you're making major changes, simplicity is a must.

5. Get Comfortable with Meal Planning and Food Prep. Plan meals so that you know what you're going to have each day, or at least have it narrowed down to a couple of options. If you work outside the home, know what meals you can bring for lunch or what options are available for a quick grab and go breakfast. Find meals that are slow-cooker friendly or easy to throw together. Actually, do this even if you don't work outside the home.

Purchase some high-quality food storage containers to hold meals that you've made ahead of time. Choose one day a week to cut and prep food for snacks and meals, then do a little batch cooking so you always have a few meal backups when things get busy, or you just don't feel like cooking.

6. Analyze Your Current Diet. It's easy to focus on all the new changes you want to make but it's hard to know how to put all of it into action if you don't know where you're starting from. Analyze your current diet by keeping track of everything you eat and drink for several days. This doesn't have to be scientific, but you do want to be thorough in your recordings.

After a few days, look at what you've eaten. Look at the individual ingredients that went into each thing you put in your mouth. By recognizing how much gluten you have in your life now, it becomes easier to eliminate it when you're ready.

7. Plan Ahead When Eating Out. This is one of those things that just catches people off guard. You're going along in your new gluten-free lifestyle and feeling great. Then suddenly someone mentions dinner in a restaurant on Friday or night or meeting with colleagues for lunch and you now feel stuck, not knowing what to do.

You can still enjoy meals out when living gluten-free. It just requires a bit more planning. I suggest you plan for this eventuality long before it happens. The first is to find out if there are any restaurants in your area that are respected for catering to special dietary needs.

Next is to look at menus from all the local restaurants and make a list of the good, the bad, and the in-between. Pour over each menu, look up the restaurant's allergen information if it's available. Have at least one or two meals picked out from each of the good or in-between restaurants. Don't even bother with the bad ones, just tell your dining companions that those are off-limits or eat before you go and enjoy a drink or coffee with them if they insist on a restaurant that doesn't meet your dietary requirements.

For added assurance, call the restaurant ahead of time to confirm that the meal you've chosen is gluten-free or that gluten-free substitutions can be made. Even restaurants that are notorious for being less than helpful in meeting special dietary needs will often be more accommodating if you give the courtesy of a phone call and a little notice.

YOUR 60 DAY, LIFE-CHANGING GLUTEN-FREE GAME PLAN

I did a lot of research before writing this book. I looked at what was already out there to help people who wanted to adopt a gluten-free lifestyle. I researched what people wanted, and what they needed. To be honest, what I found was a bit unsettling.

Millions of people are living with some degree of sensitivity or full-blown intolerance to gluten. Many of these people recognize that completely eliminating gluten from their life could improve their health in many ways. Those with Celiac disease have been forced into adapting but so many others have become lost on the concept of "how".

Change isn't easy, even when it is a change that you truly want. Shedding old habits and replacing them with healthier ones is difficult. What bothered me when I began seriously looking at what was available for people who wanted to make this significant change in their lives was that there's such a tremendous focus on instant gratification.

I'm not just talking about becoming gluten-free but rather about making any type of successful, meaningful changes to improve one's health. So many plans have catchy and intriguing titles that focus on short term results. Plans to be completed in 7 days, 14 days, or even a month. I know you want change in your life, but there isn't a magic bullet that will make it happen in only a week or two.

Real change takes longer, and I feel that this is why so many are unsuccessful and continually slip back into their old, unhealthy habits. We've been conditioned in a way to believe that we can have the change we desire quickly. If we put in a week or two of grueling work, we'll reap the benefits we deserve and live happily ever after.

As much as I wish this were true, it isn't. I'm honestly saddened when I see someone continually suffer from their health when they have the ability to take control. I don't put the blame entirely on them either. When all you see are instant fixes, this is going to be what you turn to first.

So, I'm going to play the role of the bad guy here for just a minute and tell you that this isn't going to be easy, and it can't happen overnight. I purposefully designed this book to provide you with a foundation of information that will give you the fuel you need to make it through a 60-day plan.

Why 60 days? Because research has told us time and again that our brains and bodies need 60 days to establish new habits. It takes 60 days for a new change or behavior to begin to feel like a normal, regular fixture in our daily lives.

Actually, the average is 66 days but who's counting? For some, it can even take a little bit longer, but 2 months seems to be the golden finish line when the changes you've made begin to solidify themselves. It's the point where you're more likely to lean on and turn to new habits than your old ones.

In a world full of quick fixes, 60 days can feel like a long time. I ask you to look at it this way. You're planning on making these changes for good, right? You want to improve your gut health and overall health by adopting a lifelong gluten-free lifestyle. If you succeed, you're going to still be doing this in 60 days anyway. The only way to get to day 100, 200, or to celebrate one year of living gluten-free is to start and then keep moving. You're not losing anything by taking the time to do this right.

I also have some good news for you. You don't have to be perfect during these 60 days. Research tells us that even if you slip up if you keep on track with making a change by the time you reach the 60-day mark you're still going to be successful. If you have severe gluten disease, I urge you to work with a health care provider who can help you stay on track. In your case, the costs are just too high for a slip-up. If you've been newly diagnosed with Celiac disease, I hope that this book has provided you with good information and that the 60-day plan will help make your transition smoother.

For those with a milder disease or people who simply want to eliminate gluten because you feel it's the best move for your health, I want you to acknowledge right now that you're human and that you don't need to be hard on yourself if you falter. I say this because so many people become discouraged when they fail to meet their own expectations, and they eventually give up altogether. You don't need to be perfect, but you do need to regain your focus and keep trying.

The 60-day plan I'm about to present to you might look a little different from other plans you've seen. I don't want to micromanage your journey. Instead, I'm laying out a blueprint for you to follow and adapt to your life as you see fit. Instead of daily menus and recipes that focus only on the foods you eat, I'd rather focus on weekly goals that address behaviors that will simplify your transition to a healthier, gluten-free life.

In this section, we're going to talk about the strategies you'll use over the next 60 days to reduce or eliminate gluten from your life.

A Journal: The Cornerstone of Your 60 Day Gluten-Free Journey

At various points in this book, I've mentioned the idea of keeping a journal. Now, I want to spend a little time talking about why a journal is such an important component of the 60 Day plan.

A journal serves several purposes. For starters, it keeps you accountable (at least honest journaling does). If you have to write something down and then have a permanent reminder, psychology tells us you're less likely to "cheat". Cheat really isn't a word I like to use here because you're making big changes and every bit of effort you put in improves your health in some way. There's no cheating, but rather opportunities to learn from mistakes and keep moving forward.

Which brings me to my next point of why a journal is important. When you stray from your gluten-free eating plan, a journal allows you to look back, recognize what led to the slip-up, and help you prevent it from happening again. You can also see what's happening with your body each time you stray, and each time you get back on track.

Journaling is also important because it helps you identify how your body reacts to certain foods. Some people can't tolerate any gluten, while others can tolerate it in certain amounts or from specific foods. Some might find those mild symptoms are worth an occasional break from gluten-free living. Others will realize that even the tiniest taste of any gluten food causes issues. It's hard to know where you are along this spectrum unless you've kept meticulous records in a journal.

I also think that a journal is great for people who haven't experienced any real discomfort in response to gluten but have researched enough to think eliminating it for a while is worth a try. It's truly amazing to see someone start on this journey out of curiosity and then 60 days later realize how much their body has changed and how incredible they feel. A journal is a wonderful tool for helping a person in this situation track the changes and see the progression towards healthiness.

There are different approaches you can take to journaling the first 60 days of your new gluten-free life. There isn't a one size fits all method here, so I want to encourage you to journal in a way that feels natural to you so that it becomes part of your daily habit and not something you resist because it feels like a chore. I'm going to break down the process of journaling over the next 60 days into 9 easy steps.

1. ***Find Your Journal:*** Your journal can be as simplistic or elaborate as you want it to be. Some of you might want to purchase a special journal to celebrate the beginning of this journey but you don't have to do this. If money is tight or you're just not into journals, a standard notebook that you devoted entirely to being gluten-free for 60 days works just as well. You also

have the option of using a digital journal instead of paper and pen. My only suggestion is that whatever type of journal you choose, it should be adaptable, and it should be easy to make lots of notes (you're probably going to end up recording more in your journal than you initially think you will).

2. *Know What You're Recording:* There are some basics you need to include in this journal for it to be successful. You should be able to devote a page/entry to each day. Basic entries include what you've eaten that day (include everything, even beverages or supplements), what time you ate, how you feel at the beginning and end of each day, and any out of the ordinary symptoms you experience.

3. *Add-In the Extras:* This is more than a physical journey, it's also a mental one. I think it's a good idea to devote a little journal space to just getting your thoughts out there. Talk about how you feel, if you're feeling discouraged, deprived, or frustrated. Also talk about the breakthrough moments, when you're proud of yourself, or the psychological benefits you've noticed along with the physical ones.

4. *Use Your Journal as a Medical Tool*: Keep track of any doctor's appointments you have, along with notes from each visit. If you have tests, log the results. If weight loss is one of your goals for living gluten-free, make a designated spot to record your weekly weigh-

ins, measurements, or whatever metrics you may be using to assess your progress toward goals.

5. ***Make Your Journal Work for You:*** Embarking on an entirely new dietary lifestyle is overwhelming. Even the smallest things like grocery shopping or packing a lunch can become burdensome. Use your journal as a resource to help you streamline most of this. For example, keep a grocery list of gluten-free staples you can refer to when shopping. Cross things off and add new ones as you begin to adapt to this lifestyle. Keep a list of your favorite vloggers/bloggers for when you need inspiration. Note which menu items are gluten-free from your favorite restaurants, and rate or review new dishes that you try at home. Having all of this in one place eliminates so much mental clutter.

6. ***Quality Over Quantity:*** There will be days when you just don't feel like doing it. You don't have to do it all every single day. What's important is that on the days when you're just not feeling it, you make a promise to yourself to spend just 5 minutes recording the details that matter. What did you eat and how do you feel? Don't feel like talking about your emotions today? That's fine. Even better if you leave yourself a little note saying you're just not into it. Even something like this could reveal a pattern of connection between mood and diet. There's nothing

wrong with simple, as long as you're focusing on what matters.

7. **Review**: At the end of the week, set aside some time to review your journal entries. Of course, you can do this more frequently if you want to or are experiencing new symptoms, especially if they are digestive related. I suggest doing this at the end of the week because sometimes it's easier to see what's going on when you're looking at a bigger picture. Maybe you had a bit of digestive upset or a headache for a day here or there but didn't think much of it. By looking at these symptoms over a week, you might realize that they're more prominent than you realized, or you may be able to pinpoint a triggering food that contains hidden gluten.

8. **Get to Know Your Body:** Each person's body can react differently to gluten, and a major challenge for you is identifying how it affects your body, not someone else's. When you're reviewing your journal, pay attention to when you note negative symptoms. This is important because for some, symptoms appear almost instantly, while another person may experience a surge of inflammation a day later. For this reason, you need to be open to different ways of interpreting your food journal. If you're not feeling right but don't see any potential culprits listed that day, take a look at the day before. Look for patterns. This will help you

better understand the different ways your body responds to gluten and the severity of your gluten sensitivity.

9. **Continue Past 60 Days:** Journaling for 60 days is the first goal here. As mentioned earlier, new habits are solidified right around the 60-day mark. You might find that journaling has become therapeutic or that you've used your journal as a tracker for medical or health reasons, and it's a good idea to keep it up. You don't have to stop at the 60-day mark if you don't want to.

TRANSITIONING ONE STEP AT A TIME

A lot can happen and change in 60 days. The goal here is that in 60 days, you'll be completely gluten-free, experiencing better health, and have eliminated all of your digestive issues. Each of you is starting from a different point, and this means you're not going to follow the exact same path.

Instead of providing a timeline to follow during the next 60 days, I want to give you steps to follow instead. This way you can spend extra time on the steps you need to do more work on, and not feel obligated to spend days or weeks on something that has little significance to you individually.

There isn't really a way to move too fast or fall behind here. The goal is to make the necessary changes and stick to them. If at the end of 60 days, you've only made it halfway to your goal, that's okay because it means that the halfway point is your new normal, or your new starting point. You've established habits and made healthy improvements. It doesn't matter if you need a little extra time to get all the way there, as long as you keep moving forward.

So, instead of breaking this down into week 1 or week 2, I've decided to go with step 1, step 2, etc. Take as much or as little time as you need with each step. By the time 60 days rolls around, I feel like you're going to have successfully met your goal as long as you stay on course.

Step 1: Start with a Complete Health Assessment

I want to stress that you shouldn't make major changes to your dietary lifestyle without first having a thorough health assessment and discussing your goals with the care provider. This can be your doctor, a nurse practitioner at a local clinic, a naturopathic doctor, or an alternative health practitioner who is trained in doing thorough health assessments, or any other type of skilled health practitioner.

This is important for identifying underlying health conditions that may contradict your dietary goals and also rule out other causes of your symptoms. Now is a good time to ask if any medications you take contain gluten, and what substitutions are available if they do. Plus, it's just a good idea to check in with a health professional at least once a year. If you have any type of test or blood work done, wait until you get the results back before going full steam into a new diet. There may be special nutritional considerations you need to keep in mind. Use the time that you're waiting to reread this book and research additional resources on your own.

Step 2: Start Planning

Some people are fortunate enough to live in areas where they have access to multiple grocery stores that sell fresh foods and plenty of gluten-free options. Unfortunately, this isn't the reality for many. Before you even start cleaning out your pantry (that's the next step), I want you to spend some time planning how you're going to make this work.

- What is your weekly grocery budget?
- Where will you shop?
- What foods do you need to eliminate from your regular grocery list?
- Do you need to meal plan and prep for busy days or to take lunch to work?
- How are you going to handle invitations to eat out?
- How will you respond when someone begins questioning your choices (we all have that person in our lives)?
- What are your ultimate health goals?
- What changes do you need to make for this to be a success?

- Are you ready to devote 60 days to make this happen?

This step is also a good time to start your journal. Documenting the planning process can be very eye-opening later on.

Step 3: Getting Others on Board

Not everyone has to worry about how others in their household or family are going to adjust to a new gluten-free lifestyle but getting others on board is important enough that it deserves its own step.

I know that for some, this step can be really hard. I cannot stress enough that it's important that you do what you need to for your health, regardless of what others think about it.

This can be especially challenging when you live with people who have zero desire to adapt their diets to being gluten-free. At the end of the day, it's their health and their choice. It's a case of letting go of what you cannot control - as long as you don't give in and undermine your own health in the process.

You might also have others who care deeply for you who just lack an understanding of what gluten can do to the body. I suggest you come prepared to answer their questions and provide resources for them to read or watch on their own. Going gluten-free might not be a revolutionary diet change but people are often unaware of how intrusive gluten is in our lives. Having these conversations is especially important if you have someone in your life that shows their love with food.

Which brings us to the topic of holidays. You might be 6 months away from the nearest holiday dinner with friends and family but now is a good time to introduce the idea that you're gluten-free. This way, you're not surprising them a few days before the holiday, and sharing the news early is also a good way to keep yourself accountable.

Sharing your home with others who consume gluten can be a huge challenge, especially if you're Celiac or experience severe digestive issues as a result of your gluten sensitivity. Cross-contamination is a major concern, and the risk is high if you haven't cleared all gluten from your home. We'll talk more about preparing your kitchen in the next step but here is where you'll want to talk to others about the risk of cross-contamination, and how not living in a completely gluten-free home means cooking separate meals, having designated utensil, designated pots and pans, designated cutting boards, and even doubles of certain foods. For example, you might enjoy peanut butter on gluten-free bread but if someone else comes along and sticks a knife in your peanut butter after it has touched regular bread, your peanut butter is now contaminated. For severe gluten disease, you really do need to take it this seriously.

If possible, get others involved in your 60-day gluten-free journey. They don't have to do the same level of work as you but if they just commit to eating the same gluten-free foods as you, there's a good chance they're going to see incredible improvements in their health. If they absolutely have to have gluten foods, urge them to consume them outside the home, or in a designated spot of the home where there's less of a concern about cross-contamination. Also, make sure they wash their hands after handling gluten foods.

Step 4: Tackling Command Central - The Kitchen

Some other gluten-free plans might suggest doing this part first because it sets you up for success. The reason I've saved this for step 4 is that I wanted to give you a chance to get some of the emotionally draining and stressful aspects of preparing for big change out of the way. I've seen too many people do the surface work, like preparing their kitchen, and then drag their feet on the hard stuff. If you've done steps 1 thru 3, by the time you're here, you're going to feel energized and ready to start setting things in motion.

I want to take a minute and acknowledge that this step can be emotionally difficult for some people. This is something concrete about ridding yourself of the foods you no longer want in your life. There's a sense of reaching the point of no return, and some people freeze a little at this point. It's normal. Give yourself time to pause and then keep moving.

This step can also be difficult if finances are tight. Getting rid of the food you've paid for when you're already on a tight budget is stressful. Buying new kitchen utensils and small appliances can quickly add up. I want to stress that gluten-free living can be done on a bargain budget and that certain kitchen supplies can be replaced one at a time. Produce can be purchased on even a tight budget, and you don't need a pantry full of fancy gluten-free flours to start with. If you're having trouble financially, reach out to local food pantries and ask them for resources that will help fill your refrigerator and pantry with fresh produce, proteins, and non-gluten grains.

As far as preparing your kitchen goes, this is a good time to go back to the beginning of this chapter and reread the tips I've provided. Of course, you're going to want to check all the labels and donate, give away, or throw away anything that contains gluten. Go through cupboards, pantry, refrigerator, freezer, and any other place you might have food stored. Do not leave anything with gluten in it, thinking that you might want to bake something for someone or will want "normal" foods around if you have dinner guests. Just get rid of it all.

As far as replacing utensils and appliances, you might need to do this over time. I suggest you start by replacing the necessities that you use most often. A new cooking utensil set can be purchased inexpensively. I suggest this because cooking utensils can be porous. There isn't a tremendous risk here, but it does exist. If you have people in your home that will be preparing foods that contain gluten, a separate set of both cooking and eating utensils is important.

As far as small appliances go, start with your toaster. No matter how thoroughly you clean a toaster that has been used to toast gluten bread, you're just not going to get all the crumbs out.

After you've cleared out and replaced what you're going to replace, do a thorough cleaning of your kitchen. Wear gloves and a mask if needed to prevent touching or inhaling crumbs of bread or powdered remnants of grains that contain gluten.

Step 5: The First Shop - Planning and Preparing

As excited as you may be to get started on this gluten-free lifestyle, if you head to the grocery store without much of an idea of what you need or want, chances are you're going to leave frustrated with a bunch of randomness in your cart. Give yourself some time to plan and prep for your first "big" grocery shop. You can do smaller grocery shops with simple gluten-free foods like produce and gluten-free proteins, so you don't go hungry in the meantime.

There are several steps to planning for your first gluten-free grocery shop. The first is to know where you're going to do your shopping (refer back to Step 2). Decide if you can do it all from one store, or if you'll have to visit more than one. But first, to do even this, you need to know what you're going to fill your cart with.

I suggest you start as simple as possible. Start with foods that are naturally gluten-free, including gluten-free grains. If you have foods that you love, see if there are gluten-free alternatives available. Maybe purchase a basic gluten-free flour mix in case you get the urge to experiment with gluten-free baking. Start with the staples plus maybe a few extras. This way, you won't be struggling every night trying to piece together a completely new dish for dinner.

Once you have your list of staples figured out, spend some time researching new dishes you might want to try or come up with a list of ideas for easy breakfasts or portable lunches. Look for easy meals - even if you're very talented in the kitchen. These first few weeks are all about making it as easy as possible on yourself as you're adapting to a new lifestyle.

Compile a list and be specific. Don't just jot down "gluten-free" grains because you might become completely overwhelmed and not remember what they are. Research specific gluten-free brands and note them by name on your list. Trust me when I say this will save you a ton of time.

Finally, give yourself extra time for those first few grocery shops. Go when you're not rushed, and preferably when the store isn't busy and filled with other cranky shoppers. Take your time, linger in the aisle, and read labels. Make the best choices and set yourself up for success.

Step 6: Spend Time Examining Other Sources of Gluten

The kitchen is hands down the most important place to start when eliminating gluten from your life. Still, you don't want to overlook all the other sources of hidden gluten that are found in non-food items.

Honestly, this step can feel a little tedious but it's necessary, especially if you have a severe reaction to gluten. Refer back to where we discussed non-food sources of gluten and do a thorough examination of those products. This includes many personal care products like shampoo, toothpaste, lotion, cosmetics, etc. You'll also want to check medications, vitamins, and supplements. If you're unsure, contact your pharmacy. The information they provide may be more reliable than from your doctor simply because this is their work. They can also help find gluten-free brands of the same medication for you.

If you have pets in the house, it's wise to consider how you'll deal with feeding and cleaning their dishes. Again, this might not be an issue if your reaction to gluten is mild. However, dust from pet food that contains gluten can easily make its way into the air and your body. Touching their dishes might cause a skin reaction in extremely sensitive individuals. Consider keeping your pet's food and dishes in an area of your home that you spend minimal time in. Even outdoors or on a porch if the weather is permitting. If you find you're sensitive to the gluten in your pet's food, use gloves and a mask when feeding them. You can ask your vet about gluten-free alternatives but there are mixed and very strong opinions on this.

Step 7: Move Beyond Your Comfort Zone

After a few weeks of living gluten-free, you might be ready to step out of your comfort zone and begin experiencing what it's like to be gluten-free out in the "real world". Once you've gotten comfortable with shopping and preparing a few staple meals, try your hand at something new.

Explore some recipes and see what happens when you get creative in the kitchen. Invite a friend over for a gluten-free meal or offer to bring a GF dish to a friend's or family gathering. Make a pan of gluten-free brownies to bring to the office, or visit a restaurant and order a gluten-free meal (study the menu first before going).

These steps are little, but they can feel daunting when you're embracing change. They're also important because you can't hide in the gluten-free haven of your home forever. Once you begin learning how to truly live while being gluten-free, the more solidified these habits become.

Step 8: One Foot in Front of the Other

The final step is simply to keep moving. Some days, hopefully many, will be easy and you'll feel great. Other days will prove to be more challenging. Once you've done everything you need to prepare and embrace this lifestyle, the only thing left to do is to just keep putting one foot in front of the other and moving forward until these changes in lifestyle and behavior become a habit.

Keep up with your journaling, find support, talk to your doctor about how you're feeling, pay attention to your body, and give yourself some grace as you're making these important changes. I promise if you keep the goal of improved health in mind, and keep putting one foot in front of the other, that you'll get there - and it's going to feel great when you do.

CHAPTER SUMMARY

In this chapter, we discussed how to take all the new information you have and use it to simplify your transition into a gluten-free lifestyle. Specifically, we have discussed:

- How change is often stressful, but you can make it easier;
- The importance of taking advantage of the tips provided in this book to simplify the process of transitioning;
- How important journaling is throughout this process;
- How it only takes about 60 days for a new habit to develop;

So, what next? It's time to take the leap, regain your health, and feel empowered.

7 DAY GLUTEN-FREE & PLANT-BASED MEAL PLAN WITH 21 RECIPES

To gain access to this chapter as a beautiful and colorful designed PDF where you will find all the recipes with colored images, then scan the QR code or use the link below. I hope you enjoy this delicious and tasteful add on.

SCAN ME

https://www.pureture.com/7-day-gf-vegan-meal-plan-21-recipes/

DAY 1

BREAKFAST: APPLE-LEMON BREAKFAST BOWL

This fresh apple-lemon breakfast bowl is beautifully flavored with dates, cinnamon, and walnuts. This breakfast is also deliciously filling and very nutritious.

INGREDIENTS:

- 4 to 5 medium apples, any variety
- 5 to 6 dates, pitted
- Juice of 1 lemon (about 3 tablespoons)
- 2 tablespoons of walnuts (about 6 walnut halves)
- ¼ teaspoon of ground cinnamon

INSTRUCTIONS:

1. Core the apples and cut into large pieces.
2. Place dates, half of the lemon juice, walnuts, cinnamon, and three quarters of the apple in the bowl of a food processor. Puree until finely ground, scraping down the sides of the bowl as needed.
3. Add the remainder of the apples and lemon juice and pulse until the apples are shredded and the date mixture is evenly distributed.

LUNCH: SPICY BUFFALO CHICKPEA WRAPS

I hope you'll love these wraps! They're:

- Savory
- Spicy
- Hearty
- Crunchy from the vegetables
- Tender from the chickpeas
- Quick
- Protein & fiber-filled
- Delicious

INGREDIENTS:

DRESSING + SALAD

- ⅓ cup of hummus (or store-bought)
- 1½ - 2 tbsp of maple syrup (plus more to taste)
- 1 small lemon, juiced (1 small lemon yields ~2 Tbsp or 30 ml)
- 1-2 tbsp of hot water (to thin)
- 1 head of romaine lettuce (or sub 1 bundle kale per 1 head romaine // cleaned, large stems removed, roughly chopped)

BUFFALO CHICKPEAS

- 1 15-ounce can of chickpeas (rinsed, drained and dried // ~ 1 ¼ cups per can when drained)
- 1 tbsp of coconut oil (or sub grape seed or olive oil)
- 4 tbsp of hot sauce (I used Louisiana's Pure Crystal Hot Sauce)
- ¼ tsp of garlic powder (or sub 1 minced garlic clove per ¼ tsp powder)
- 1 pinch of sea salt

FOR SERVING AND TOPPINGS

- 3-4 corn tortillas, gluten-free pita, or gluten-free flatbread
- ¼ cup of red onion, diced (optional)
- ¼ cup of baby tomato, diced (optional)
- ¼ ripe avocado, thinly sliced (optional)

INSTRUCTIONS:

1. Make dressing by adding hummus, maple syrup, and lemon juice to a mixing bowl and whisking to combine. Add hot water until thick but pourable.
2. Taste and adjust flavor as needed, then add romaine lettuce or kale, and toss. Set aside.
3. To make chickpeas, add drained, dried chickpeas to a

separate mixing bowl. Add coconut oil, 3 Tbsp hot sauce, garlic powder, and a pinch of salt - toss to combine/coat.
4. Heat a metal or cast-iron skillet over medium heat. Once hot, add chickpeas and sauté for 3-5 minutes, mashing a few chickpeas gently with a spoon to create texture.
5. Once chickpeas are hot and slightly dried out, remove from heat and add remaining 1 Tbsp of hot sauce. Stir to combine. Set aside.
6. To assemble, top each wrap with a generous portion of the dressed romaine salad, and top with ¼ cup of buffalo chickpeas and a sprinkle of diced tomatoes, avocado, and/or onion (optional).
7. Serve immediately. Store leftovers separately in the refrigerator up to 3 days, though best when fresh. You can enjoy the buffalo chickpeas cold, room temperature or heated up.

DINNER: ROASTED CAULIFLOWER AND QUINOA CASSEROLE

This easy, cozy casserole melds tender quinoa with roasted cauliflower, green peas, and a zesty marinara sauce.

INGREDIENTS:

- 2 cups of dry quinoa

- 3½ cups of vegetable broth, divided
- ½ medium onion, cut into ¼-inch dice (1 cup)
- 6 cloves of garlic, minced
- 1 tablespoon of Italian seasoning
- 1 medium head of cauliflower, cut into 1-inch florets (about 6 cups)
- 1 tablespoon of white wine vinegar
- Sea salt and freshly ground black pepper
- 3 cups of store-bought marinara sauce
- 1 cup of frozen green peas, thawed

INSTRUCTIONS:

1. In a large saucepan, combine quinoa and 3 cups of broth. Bring to a boil; then reduce heat to low and cover pan. Simmer for 20 minutes. Remove from heat and let it stand for 10 minutes. Drain off any excess water if needed.
2. In a skillet, combine onion, garlic, Italian seasoning, and ¼ cup broth; cook over medium for 10 minutes or until onion is tender, adding more broth, 1 to 2 tablespoons at a time, as needed to prevent sticking. Add cauliflower to skillet and cook 10 to 15 minutes more, or until cauliflower is starting to get tender. Do not overcook. Add vinegar and season with salt and pepper.
3. Preheat oven to 350°F. Fluff quinoa with a fork; then

spread it in an even layer on the bottom of a large casserole dish. Cover quinoa with an even layer of marinara sauce, followed by cauliflower and green peas on top. Bake uncovered 20 to 25 minutes until there is browning on the cauliflower. Serve warm.

BREAKFAST: CAULIFLOWER BREAKFAST SCRAMBLE

There are many very good recipes for scrambles, but most call for tofu. In this recipe, cauliflower takes the place of the tofu—with delicious results.

INGREDIENTS:

- 1 red onion, peeled and cut into ½-inch dice
- 1 red bell pepper, seeded and cut into ½-inch dice
- 1 green bell pepper, seeded and cut into ½-inch dice
- 2 cups of sliced mushrooms (from about 8 ounces whole mushrooms)
- 1 large head of cauliflower, cut into florets, or 2 (19-ounce) cans ackee, drained and gently rinsed
- Sea salt
- ½ teaspoon of freshly ground black pepper
- 1½ teaspoons of turmeric
- ¼ teaspoon of cayenne pepper, or to taste
- 3 cloves of garlic, peeled and minced
- 1 to 2 tablespoons of low-sodium soy sauce

- ¼ cup of nutritional yeast (optional)

INSTRUCTIONS:

1. Place the onion, red and green peppers, and mushrooms in a medium skillet or saucepan and sauté over medium-high heat for 7 to 8 minutes, or until the onion is translucent. Add 1 to 2 tablespoons of water at a time to keep the vegetables from sticking to the pan.
2. Add the cauliflower and cook for 5 to 6 minutes, or until the florets are tender.
3. Add the salt to taste, pepper, turmeric, cayenne, garlic, soy sauce, and nutritional yeast (if using) to the pan, and cook for 5 minutes more, or until hot and fragrant.

LUNCH: 5 MINUTE VEGGIE COCONUT WRAPS

Not only are they easy to make, requiring just **8 ingredients** and **5 minutes** to prepare, they are the ideal easy lunch or snack!

These are:

- Crunchy
- Flavor-packed
- Loaded with vegetables
- Fiber & Protein-rich
- Quick & easy

- Ridiculously delicious

INGREDIENTS:

- 5 Coconut Wraps (I love the Nuco Brand in turmeric flavor)
- ⅔ cup of hummus
- 7 ½ tbsp of green curry paste
- 1 red bell pepper - thinly sliced
- 1 cup of fresh cilantro (approximately 1 large bundle)
- 1 ½ cups of shredded carrots
- 1 ripe avocado - sliced
- 2 ½ cups of kale - chopped

INSTRUCTIONS:

1. Lay a single coconut wrap on a clean surface or cutting board. Add 2 Tbsp (~32 g) hummus and 1 ½ Tbsp curry paste (~22 g) and spread on the end of the wrap closest to you.
2. Add bell pepper, carrots, avocado, kale, and cilantro and roll tightly away from you. Place the seam side down on a serving platter. Repeat until you have 5 coconut wraps (or as many as you desire).
3. Best served fresh. Can store leftovers covered in the refrigerator up to 1 day.

DINNER: WHITE BEAN FETTUCCINE ALFREDO WITH PEAS AND SUN-DRIED TOMATOES

Fettuccine Alfredo has never been the healthiest pasta choice until now. In this version, a blended white bean sauce is used instead of cream, dried tomatoes take the place of bacon, and fresh sugar snap peas add more of a crunch and flavor than petite green peas.

INGREDIENTS:

- 8 oz. of dry gluten-free fettuccine
- 8 oz. sugar snap peas, halved
- 1 15-oz. can of cannellini beans, rinsed and drained (1½ cups)
- 2 cloves of garlic
- 2 tablespoons of nutritional yeast
- 2 tablespoons of almond butter
- ⅓ cup of ready-to-eat sun-dried tomatoes, thinly sliced
- Sea salt and freshly ground black pepper to taste

INSTRUCTIONS:

1. Cook fettuccine according to package directions for al dente, adding peas the last 3 minutes of cooking. Drain, reserving ¾ cup cooking liquid.
2. Meanwhile, in a food processor, combine beans, garlic,

nutritional yeast, and almond butter. Process until smooth. Add the reserved cooking liquid; process until smooth.

3. Return pasta and peas to the pot. Stir in bean sauce and tomatoes. Season with salt and pepper.

BREAKFAST: HEALTHY OATMEAL WITH FRUIT AND NUTS

Oatmeal is one of my favorite breakfast foods. It is quick to prepare and easily adaptable to my ever-changing moods—some days I want it with fruit, some days I want it plain, and sometimes I want a little bit of everything in it (that's when I include all of the optional ingredients listed here!). This basic recipe is all you need to get started … add as much or as little of the extras as you like.

INGREDIENTS:

- ¾ cup of gluten-free rolled oats
- ¼ teaspoon of ground cinnamon
- Pinch of sea salt
- ¼ cup of fresh berries (optional)
- ½ ripe banana, sliced (optional)
- 2 tablespoons of chopped nuts, such as walnuts, pecans, or cashews (optional)
- 2 tablespoons of dried fruit, such as raisins, cranberries, chopped apples, chopped

- Apricots (optional)
- Maple syrup (optional)

INSTRUCTIONS:

1. Combine the oats and 1½ cups water in a small saucepan. Bring to a boil over high heat. Reduce the heat to medium-low and cook until the water has been absorbed, about 5 minutes.
2. Stir in the cinnamon and salt. Top with the berries, banana, nuts, and/or dried fruit, as you like. If desired, pour a little maple syrup on top. Serve hot.

LUNCH: ABUNDANCE KALE SALAD WITH SAVORY TAHINI DRESSING

An abundant kale salad with roasted sweet potato, zucchini, avocado, sprouts, crispy chickpeas, and kimchi! Topped with a savory tahini dressing, this salad makes the perfect 30-minute meal or side.

INGREDIENTS:

ROASTED VEGETABLES

- 1 medium zucchini (sliced in ¼-inch rounds)
- 1 medium sweet potato (sliced in ¼-inch rounds)
- 1 cup of red cabbage (shredded)

- 1 tbsp of melted coconut oil or sub water)
- 1 pinch of sea salt
- ½ tsp DIY curry powder (or store-bought)

DRESSING

- ⅓ cup of tahini
- ½ tsp of garlic powder (plus more to taste)
- 1 tbsp of coconut aminos (plus more to taste or sub tamari or soy sauce)
- 1 pinch of sea salt (omit if using tamari or soy sauce, as the flavor is more intense)
- 1 large clove of garlic (minced)
- ¼ cup of water (to thin)

SALAD

- 6 cups of mixed greens (kale, romaine, mixed greens, etc.)
- 4 small radishes (thinly sliced)
- 3 tbsp of hemp seeds
- 1 ripe avocado (cubed)
- 2 tbsp of lemon juice or apple cider vinegar

TOPPINGS optional / choose your favorites

- 1 batch of crispy baked chickpeas

- 2 cups of cooked quinoa
- DIY Kimchi (or store-bought)

INSTRUCTIONS:

1. If serving with quinoa or crispy chickpeas, prepare at this time. Otherwise, proceed to step 2.
2. Preheat the oven to 375 degrees F (190 C) and arrange zucchini, cabbage, and sweet potatoes on a baking sheet (one or more as needed). Drizzle with coconut oil (or sub oil-free options), sea salt, and curry powder and toss to combine. Roast for 20 minutes or until tender and slightly golden brown.
3. In the meantime, prepare dressing by adding tahini, garlic powder, coconut aminos, sea salt, and garlic to a small mixing bowl and whisking to combine. Then add enough water to thin until pourable and whisk until smooth. Taste and adjust seasonings as needed, adding more garlic powder for garlic flavor, coconut aminos for depth of flavor, or salt for saltiness. Set aside.
4. Assemble salad by adding greens, radishes, hemp seeds, and avocado to a large mixing bowl. Add the lemon juice (or apple cider vinegar) and gently toss to combine.
5. Add roasted vegetables and any other desired toppings (quinoa, chickpeas, etc.) and serve with dressing.
6. Best when fresh, though leftovers keep well stored in

the refrigerator up to 3 days. Dressing stored separately will keep for 7 days. Chickpeas should be stored separately at room temperature to maintain crispiness.

DINNER: LEMON BROCCOLI ROTINI

Enjoy the classic combination of broccoli, lemon, and tarragon in this creamy pasta dish. For the best presentation, use the same half of the lemon for the zest and juice, reserving the other half to cut into wedges for serving.

INGREDIENTS:

- 3 cups of sliced cremini mushrooms (8 oz.)
- 1 medium onion, chopped (1 cup)
- 4 cloves of garlic, minced
- 4 cups of dried gluten-free rotini pasta (12 oz.)
- 2 cups of low-sodium vegetable broth
- 2 cups of unsweetened, unflavored plant-based milk
- 1 lemon
- 1 16-oz. package of frozen of broccoli florets (or 6 cups fresh)
- ½ cup of chopped roasted red bell peppers
- 1 teaspoon of chopped fresh tarragon
- Sea salt and freshly ground black pepper, to taste

INSTRUCTIONS:

1. In a large saucepan cook mushrooms, onion, and garlic over medium 2 to 3 minutes, stirring occasionally and adding water, 1 to 2 Tbsp. at a time, as needed to prevent sticking. Stir in rotini, vegetable broth, and milk. Bring to boiling; reduce heat. Cover and simmer for 5 to 7 minutes or as specified on the pasta box until pasta is nearly tender.
2. Remove 1 tsp. zest from lemon and stir into a saucepan with pasta. Stir in broccoli, red peppers, and tarragon. Cook for about 5 minutes or until broccoli and pasta are tender. Stir in 1 Tbsp. of juice from lemon. Season with salt and black pepper. If desired, sprinkle with additional lemon zest and serve with lemon wedges.

BREAKFAST: CHICKPEA OMELET

This wonderful egg-free omelet is easy to make and is delicious for breakfast, lunch, or dinner.

INGREDIENTS:

- 1 cup of chickpea flour
- ½ teaspoon of onion powder
- ½ teaspoon of garlic powder
- ¼ teaspoon of white pepper
- ¼ teaspoon of black pepper

- ⅓ cup of nutritional yeast
- ½ teaspoon of baking soda
- 3 green onions (white and green parts), chopped
- 4 ounces of sautéed mushrooms (optional)

INSTRUCTIONS:

1. Combine the chickpea flour, onion powder, garlic powder, white pepper, black pepper, nutritional yeast, and baking soda in a small bowl. Add 1 cup of water and stir until the batter is smooth.
2. Heat a frying pan over medium heat. Pour the batter into the pan, as if making pancakes. Sprinkle 1 to 2 tablespoons of the green onions and mushrooms into the batter for each omelet as it cooks. Flip the omelet. When the underside is browned, flip the omelet again, and cook the other side for a minute.
3. Serve your amazing Chickpea Omelet topped with tomatoes, spinach, salsa, hot sauce, or whatever heart-safe, plant-perfect fixings you like.

LUNCH: ROASTED RAINBOW VEGETABLE BOWL

This is a healthy, easy, and delicious roasted vegetable bowl with tahini dressing and hemp seeds! The perfect 30-minute plant-based meal for any time of the day!

INGREDIENTS:

VEGETABLES

- 3-4 medium red or yellow baby potatoes (sliced into ¼ -inch rounds)
- ½ of a large sweet potato (skin on // sliced into ¼ -inch rounds)
- 2 large carrots (halved and thinly sliced)
- 1 medium beet (sliced into ⅛ -inch rounds)
- 4 medium radishes (halved, or quartered if large)
- 2 tbsp of avocado or melted coconut oil
- 1 tsp of curry powder
- ½ tsp of sea salt (divided)
- 1 cup of cabbage (thinly sliced)
- 1 medium red pepper (thinly sliced)
- 1 cup of broccolini (roughly chopped)
- 2 cups of chopped collard greens or kale (organic when possible)

TOPPINGS

- 1 medium lemon (juiced or 3 Tbsp store bought lemon juice)
- 2 tbsp of tahini (divided)
- 2 tbsp of hemp seeds (divided)
- ½ of a medium avocado (divided // optional)

INSTRUCTIONS:

1. Preheat the oven to 400 degrees F (204 C) and line two baking sheets with parchment paper (or more baking sheets if increasing batch size).
2. To one baking sheet, add the potatoes, sweet potatoes, carrots, beets, and radishes and drizzle with half of the oil (or water), curry powder, and sea salt Toss to combine. Bake for 20-25 minutes or until golden brown and tender.
3. To the second baking sheet, add the cabbage, bell pepper, and broccolini. Drizzle with the remaining half of the oil (or water), curry powder, and sea salt. Toss to combine.
4. When the potatoes/carrots hit the 10-minute mark, add the second pan to the oven and bake for a total of 15-20 minutes. In the last 5 minutes of baking, add the collard greens or kale to either pan and roast until tender and bright green.
5. To serve, divide vegetables between serving plates and garnish with avocado (optional) and season with lemon juice, tahini, hemp seeds, and another pinch of sea salt (optional). You could also garnish with any fresh herbs you have!
6. Best when fresh. Store leftovers covered in the refrigerator for 3-4 days. Reheat in a 350-degree F (176

C) oven or on the stovetop over medium heat until hot.

DINNER: GARLICKY BOK CHOY NOODLE SOUP

The vegetables in this colorful noodle soup are just barely cooked, so they stay crisp in texture and bright in color. Baby bok choy, harvested when it's about 6 inches long, is milder and more tender than mature bok choy.

INGREDIENTS:

- 4 cups of no-salt-added vegetable broth
- 4 cloves of garlic, minced
- 1 tablespoons of minced fresh ginger
- 2 teaspoons of reduced-sodium soy sauce
- 6 ounces of dried brown rice (gluten-free) pad Thai noodles
- 12 baby carrots with green tops, halved lengthwise, or 2 cups bias-sliced carrots
- 3 ounces of extra-firm light silken-style tofu, cut into ¼-inch cubes
- 2 heads of baby bok choy, halved lengthwise
- 12 thin spears asparagus, trimmed
- 1 cup of fresh shiitake mushrooms, stems removed, or oyster mushrooms, sliced

- 4 scallions (green onions), green tops trimmed and cut in half lengthwise
- 1 lime, cut into wedges

INSTRUCTIONS:

1. In a 5- to 6-qt. pot, combine 4 cups of water, the broth, garlic, ginger, and soy sauce. Bring to boiling; reduce heat. Cover and simmer for 10 minutes to allow flavors to meld.
2. Add noodles, carrots, and tofu. Simmer, uncovered, 8 minutes, stirring occasionally. Add bok choy, asparagus, mushrooms, and scallions. Simmer, uncovered, 1 minute more. Serve in shallow bowls with lime wedges.

BREAKFAST: CHOCOLATE CHIP COCONUT PANCAKES

These pancakes are so simple and delicious, and they're just as good for dessert as they are for breakfast! Plus, they freeze really well, so you can make an extra batch and freeze them. Use a large griddle so that you can cook three or four at a time.

INGREDIENTS:

- 1 tablespoon of flaxseed meal
- 1¼ cups of gluten-free buckwheat flour

- ¼ cup of old-fashioned rolled oats
- 2 tablespoons of unsweetened coconut flakes
- 1 tablespoon of baking powder
- Pinch of sea salt
- 1 cup of unsweetened, unflavored plant milk
- ½ cup of unsweetened applesauce
- ¼ cup of pure maple syrup
- 1 teaspoon of pure vanilla extract
- ⅓ cup of grain-sweetened, vegan mini chocolate chips
- Sliced bananas, for serving

INSTRUCTIONS:

1. Place the flaxseed meal in a small saucepan with ½ cup water. Cook over medium heat until the mixture gets a little sticky and appears stringy when it drips off a spoon, 3 to 4 minutes. Immediately strain the mixture into a glass measuring cup and set aside. Discard the seeds.
2. In a large bowl, whisk together the GF buckwheat flour, oats, coconut flakes, baking powder, and salt.
3. In a medium bowl, whisk together the milk, applesauce, maple syrup, vanilla, and 2 tablespoons of the reserved flax water.
4. Add the liquid mixture to the dry mix and stir together to blend; the batter will be thick. Stir in the chocolate chips.

5. Heat a nonstick griddle over medium-low heat. Pour ⅓ cup batter for each pancake onto the griddle and spread gently. Cook for 6 to 8 minutes, until the pancakes look slightly dry on top, are lightly browned on the bottom, and release easily from the pan. Flip and cook for about 5 minutes on the other side.
6. Repeat for the remaining batter, wiping off the griddle between batches. Serve hot with sliced bananas.

Storage: Place cooked pancakes in an airtight container and refrigerate for up to 5 days or frozen for up to 1 month. Reheat pancakes in a 350°F oven for 15 minutes for refrigerated pancakes and 25 minutes if frozen.

LUNCH: VEGAN "BLT" SANDWICH

6-Ingredient vegan "BLT" sandwich made with vegan mayo and eggplant bacon! Crisp, smoky, flavorful, and so delicious.

INGREDIENTS:

- 2 slices of gluten-free, vegan bread
- 5-6 slices of eggplant bacon or ¼ cup of coconut bacon
- 2 tbsp of Vegan mayo or hummus
- ¼ medium red or white onion (thinly sliced)
- ½ medium ripe tomato (thinly sliced)
- 2 leaves of green lettuce

INSTRUCTIONS:

1. Toast bread (optional). In the meantime, heat skillet over medium heat. Once hot, add eggplant bacon (if using coconut bacon, no need to heat) and cook for 1-2 minutes. Then flip and cook for another 1-2 minutes on the other side until warmed through. Remove from heat and set aside.
2. To assemble the sandwich, spread vegan mayo (or hummus) on the toasted bread slices. Then top one piece with Eggplant or Coconut Bacon, onion, tomato, and lettuce. Top with another piece of bread, slice (optional), and enjoy.
3. Could be made ahead of time (up to a few hours), but best when fresh.

DINNER: ROASTED VEGGIE FLATBREADS

Balsamic glaze is the perfect finishing touch for these flatbreads. When making it, watch carefully at the end so it doesn't scorch.

INGREDIENTS:

- Cornmeal, for dusting
- 1 recipe of homemade, oil free, gluten-free pizza dough (or store bought)
- 6 baby potatoes, quartered
- 8 Brussels sprouts, quartered

- 1 medium carrot, coarsely chopped
- 1 medium shallot, coarsely chopped
- 1 tablespoon of red wine vinegar
- Sea salt and freshly ground black pepper, to taste
- ⅓ cup of balsamic vinegar
- 1 cup of no-salt-added canned cannellini beans, rinsed and drained
- 1 teaspoon of finely chopped fresh sage or ¼ tsp. dried sage, crushed
- 2 cups of fresh microgreen

INSTRUCTIONS:

1. Preheat the oven to 400°F. Lightly sprinkle a large baking sheet with cornmeal.
2. Divide dough into four portions. On a lightly gluten-free floured surface, roll portions into 7- to 8-inch circles or 10×5-inch ovals. Transfer flatbreads to the prepared pan. Bake 10 to 13 minutes or until lightly browned and set (flatbreads may puff). Let cool.
3. Preheat the oven to 425°F. Line a 15×10-inch baking pan with foil. Arrange potatoes, Brussels sprouts, carrot, and shallot in a prepared baking pan. Sprinkle with red wine vinegar and season with salt and pepper. Roast about 20 minutes or until tender and lightly browned.
4. Meanwhile, for balsamic glaze, in a small saucepan

bring balsamic vinegar to boiling; reduce heat. Simmer, uncovered, about 6 minutes or until mixture has reduced to about 1 ½ Tbsp. and thickened to a syrup consistency.

5. In a bowl, mash beans with a fork and stir in sage and 2 tsp of water. Spread on flatbreads. Top with roasted vegetables. Remove foil from baking sheet; transfer flatbreads to baking sheet. Bake for 5 minutes to heat through.
6. Drizzle flatbreads with balsamic glaze and top with microgreens.

BREAKFAST: BLACK BEAN AND SWEET POTATO HASH

This black bean and sweet potato hash can be an ideal breakfast, a lunch, or a light dinner. It can be served simply as a side dish, spooned over brown rice or quinoa, wrapped in a gluten-free tortilla, or made into soft tacos garnished with avocado, cilantro, and other favorite toppings. Make it in your Instant Pot or other pressure cooker, or do it the old-fashioned way, on the stovetop.

INGREDIENTS:

- 1 cup of chopped onion
- 1 to 2 cloves of garlic, minced

- 2 cups of chopped peeled sweet potatoes (about 2 small or medium)
- 2 teaspoons of mild or hot chili powder
- ⅓ cup of low-sodium vegetable broth
- 1 cup of cooked black beans
- ¼ cup of chopped scallions
- Splash of hot sauce (optional)
- Chopped cilantro, for garnish

INSTRUCTIONS:

Stovetop Method

1. Place the onions in a nonstick skillet and sauté over medium heat, stirring occasionally, for 2 to 3 minutes. Add the garlic and stir.
2. Add the sweet potatoes and chili powder, and stir to coat the vegetables with the chili powder. Add broth and stir. Cook for about 12 minutes more, stirring occasionally, until the potatoes are cooked through. Add more liquid - 1 to 2 tablespoons at a time as needed, to keep the vegetables from sticking to the pan.
3. Add the black beans, scallions, and salt. Cook for 1 or 2 minutes more, until the beans are heated through.
4. Add the hot sauce (if using), and stir. Taste and adjust the seasonings. Top with chopped cilantro and serve.

Pressure Cooker Method

1. Heat a stovetop pressure cooker over medium heat or set an electric cooker to sauté. Add the onion and cook, stirring occasionally, for 2 to 3 minutes. Add the garlic and stir. Add the sweet potatoes and chili powder. Stir to coat the sweet potatoes with the chili powder. Add the broth and stir.
2. Lock the lid on the pressure cooker. Bring to high pressure for 3 minutes. Quick release the pressure. Remove the lid, tilting it away from you.
3. Add the black beans, scallions, and salt. Cook for 1 or 2 minutes more over medium heat, or lock on the lid for 3 minutes, until the beans are heated through.
4. Add the hot sauce (if using), and stir. Taste and adjust the seasonings. Top with chopped cilantro and serve.

LUNCH: CURRIED CAULIFLOWER, GRAPE & LENTIL SALAD

This crazy delicious kale salad is topped with red grapes, lentils, and curry roasted cauliflower. Served with a tahini-green curry paste dressing! Just 30 minutes required for this flavorful side or entrée.

INGREDIENTS:

CAULIFLOWER

- 1 head of cauliflower (divided into florets)
- 1 ½ tbsp of melted coconut oil (or water)
- 1 ½ tbsp of curry powder (or store-bought)
- ¼ tsp sea salt

GREEN CURRY TAHINI DRESSING*

- 4 ½ tbsp of green curry paste (or store-bought, though fresh is best)
- 2 tbsp of tahini
- 2 tbsp of lemon juice
- 1 tbsp of maple syrup
- 1 Pinch each of salt and black pepper
- Water to thin

SALAD

- 5-6 cups of mixed greens, kale, spinach (or other green of choice)
- 1 cup of cooked lentils (rinsed and drained)
- 1 cup of red or green grapes (halved)
- Fresh cilantro (optional)

INSTRUCTIONS:

1. Preheat the oven to 400 degrees F (204 C). Line a baking sheet (or more as needed) with parchment paper.
2. Add cauliflower to a mixing bowl and toss with coconut oil (or water), curry powder, and sea salt. Transfer to a baking sheet and roast cauliflower for 20-25 minutes or until golden brown and tender.
3. Prepare dressing by adding green curry paste, tahini, lemon juice, maple syrup, salt, and pepper to a mixing bowl and whisking to combine. If needed, thin with water until pourable.
4. Taste and adjust flavor as needed, adding more green curry paste for a stronger curry flavor, tahini for greater thickness, lemon juice for acidity, or maple syrup for sweetness.
5. Assemble salad by adding lettuce to a serving platter or bowl. Top with lentils, grapes, and cooked cauliflower and serve with dressing. Optional: garnish with fresh cilantro.
6. Best served fresh. Store leftovers in an airtight container for 3-4 days. Store dressing separately for up to 1 week.

DINNER: SPAGHETTI MARINARA WITH LENTIL BALLS

This whole-food vegan take on classic spaghetti and meatballs is as healthy as it is satisfying. The lentil "meatballs" take some time to make, but they're well worth the effort. They also freeze beautifully for up to a month: After baking, freeze them in an airtight container. Reheat in a 350°F oven 20 to 30 minutes.

INGREDIENTS:

- 1 cup of dry brown lentils, rinsed and drained
- 1 8-oz. package of button or cremini mushrooms, trimmed and chopped
- 1 onion, chopped (1 cup)
- 3 small cloves of garlic, minced
- ½ cup of gluten-free flour
- 3 tablespoons of reduced-sodium tamari or soy sauce
- 2 tablespoons of no-salt-added tomato paste
- 1 tablespoon of nutritional yeast
- 1 teaspoon of dried oregano, crushed
- 1 teaspoon of onion powder
- Sea salt and freshly ground black pepper, to taste
- 1 lb. of dry gluten-free spaghetti
- 6 cups of oil-free marinara sauce
- 2 Tbsp. of chopped fresh basil

INSTRUCTIONS:

1. In a large saucepan combine lentils and 1 cup of water. Bring to boiling; reduce heat. Cover and simmer for 15 minutes. Add mushrooms, onion, and garlic. Cover and cook about 15 minutes more or until lentils are tender. Uncover and cook until any remaining liquid has evaporated.
2. Stir in the next seven ingredients (through salt and pepper). Cook, uncovered, over low about 10 minutes or until liquid is absorbed and the pan is very dry, stirring occasionally. (Watch carefully so lentils do not scorch.) Spread mixture in a shallow baking pan; cool completely.
3. Preheat the oven to 250°F. Line a 15×10-inch baking pan with parchment paper. Scoop out 2 Tbsp. lentil mixture, shape into a ball, and place in the prepared pan. Repeat to make about 20 lentil balls. Bake for 45 minutes or until lightly browned and crisp.
4. Meanwhile, cook spaghetti according to package directions. In a saucepan heat marinara sauce. Drain spaghetti, return to pot, and toss with 3 cups of the warm marinara sauce.
5. To serve, top spaghetti with lentil balls and top with the remaining sauce. Sprinkle with basil.

BREAKFAST: EASY OVERNIGHT OATS WITH CHIA

To get through those busy weeks, try this easy and healthy breakfast that you can make the night before.

INGREDIENTS:

- ¾ cup of gluten-free rolled oats
- ¼ cup of plant milk
- ½ cup of water
- 1 heaping tablespoon of chia seeds
- ½-1 tablespoon of maple syrup
- ¼ teaspoon of cinnamon
- Dash of vanilla bean powder or extract
- Fruit of choice

INSTRUCTIONS:

1. Place oats, liquid, chia seeds, maple syrup, cinnamon, and vanilla into a 16-ounce mason jar or container of choice. Mix well. Seal shut and place the jar in the refrigerator overnight.
2. In the morning, mix again and top with anything you'd like, such as fresh fruit, more chia seeds, or cacao nibs.

LUNCH: CHICKPEA QUINOA SALAD WITH ORANGE SOY & SESAME DRESSING

This hearty salad is absolutely loaded with good-for-you ingredients like chickpeas, quinoa, pumpkin seeds, sesame seeds, hemp seeds, kale, nutritional yeast, garlic, ginger, red and green bell peppers (just to name a few!) You can make this salad with quinoa or couscous. Quinoa has slightly more protein and quite a bit more fibre than couscous, but couscous is easier to prepare and cooks more quickly.

INGREDIENTS:

ORANGE SOY & SESAME DRESSING

- 1 navel orange, juiced
- 1 tbsp of sesame oil
- 1 tbsp of canola oil
- 1 tbsp of agave syrup
- 2 tbsp of soy sauce
- ½ tbsp of rice wine vinegar
- 1 ½ tbsp of nutritional yeast
- 2 cloves of garlic, minced
- ½" chunk of ginger, minced
- 1 tbsp of sesame seeds

CHICKPEA QUINOA SALAD

- 3 cups of quinoa, cooked (cook in broth for best flavour)
- 1 (540ml/19 fl. oz.) can of chickpeas, drained (approx. 2 cups cooked)
- ⅔ cup of chopped kale (stems removed, packed)
- ½ cup of chopped red and green bell pepper
- ¼ cup of chopped green onion
- ¼ cup of raw pumpkin seeds
- 2-4 tbsp of hemp hearts

INSTRUCTIONS:

ORANGE SOY & SESAME DRESSING

1. Combine all ingredients. Mix well and set aside.

CHICKPEA & QUINOA SALAD

1. If not already chilled, refrigerate cooked quinoa.
2. While the quinoa chills, combine kale with orange soy & sesame dressing. Set aside.
3. Combine room temperature (or cooler) quinoa, kale, dressing, and all remaining ingredients.
4. Refrigerate until chilled before serving.

DINNER: "STUFFINGED" SWEET POTATOES

These scrumptious stuffed sweet potatoes are worthy of center stage on a holiday table. Cremini mushrooms and chickpeas add lusciousness to a classic bread stuffing that is loaded with traditional flavor. This recipe requires only about 30 minutes of active prep time.

Tip: To dry bread cubes, spread them in a single layer in a baking pan. Let stand, uncovered, overnight. Or bake in a 300°F oven 10 to 15 minutes or until golden, stirring once or twice.

INGREDIENTS:

- 4 large sweet potatoes, scrubbed and patted dry (about 3 lb.)
- 1½ cups of chopped fresh cremini mushrooms (4 oz.)
- ½ cup of chopped onion
- 2 stalks of celery, sliced (½ cup)
- 2 cloves of garlic, minced
- 2 15-oz. cans of no-salt-added chickpeas, rinsed and drained
- 2 cups of ½-inch gluten-free bread cubes, dried (see tip in intro)
- ½ cup of chopped fresh parsley
- 1½ teaspoon of poultry seasoning
- Sea salt and freshly ground black pepper, to taste
- ¼ to ⅓ cup of low-sodium vegetable broth

INSTRUCTIONS:

1. Preheat the oven to 400°F. Prick sweet potatoes all over with a fork. Place in a 3-qt. rectangular baking dish. Bake about 45 minutes or until just tender when pierced with a knife. Let stand until cool enough to handle.
2. Meanwhile, for stuffing, in a large nonstick skillet cook mushrooms, onion, celery, and garlic over medium 5 minutes, stirring occasionally and adding water, 1 to 2 Tbsp. at a time, as needed to prevent sticking.
3. In a food processor combine mushroom mixture and chickpeas; pulse until chopped. Transfer to a bowl. Add bread cubes, parsley, poultry seasoning, salt, and pepper. Drizzle with broth, tossing just until moistened.
4. Cut sweet potatoes in half lengthwise. Using a sharp knife, score around potato flesh, leaving a ¼-inch shell and being careful not to cut through skin. Score in a crisscross to make ½-inch cubes. Gently scoop cubes out with a spoon. If necessary, cut any large pieces in half to make smaller cubes. Add cubes to the stuffing mixture in a bowl; gently fold to combine.
5. Arrange potato skin shells in the baking dish. Spoon stuffing into shells. Bake, uncovered, about 20 minutes or until browned and heated through. To transport,

place the baking dish in an insulated carrier with a hot pack.

CHAPTER SUMMARY

In this last chapter, we provided you with a 7 day gluten-free and plant-based meal plan consisting of 3 meals per day. Specifically, we've shared:

- Breakfast recipes for 7 days;
- Lunch recipes for 7 days;
- Dinner recipes for 7 days;
- A total of 21 recipes to get you started in the right direction of adopting more of a gluten-free and plant-based lifestyle.

With everything you've learned, you're ready to take the first steps toward eliminating pain and reclaiming your gut health by taking a gluten-free and plant-based approach. Start with the given meal plan and play around along the way. I have all the confidence in the world that you can do this.

192 | THE GLUTEN-FREE GUT HEALTH PLAN & COOKBOOK ...

To gain access to this chapter as a beautiful and colorful designed PDF where you will find all the recipes with colored images, then scan the QR code or use the link below. I hope you enjoy this delicious and tasteful add on.

SCAN ME

https://www.pureture.com/7-day-gf-vegan-meal-plan-21-recipes/

CONCLUSION

You have made an important first step in improving your health. Millions of people around the globe suffer from gluten-related health problems. Starting today, you will no longer be one of them.

For some people, gluten is nothing short of devastating to their health. For many others, gluten slowly and quietly damages their health until it reaches a point it can no longer be ignored. Digestive issues are one of the main symptoms of gluten-sensitivity or intolerance but that's far from the extent of damage that gluten can do.

My goal with this book has been to provide you with a framework of knowledge to help you better understand what gluten is, the many effects it can have on your health, and how to successfully reduce consumption or even remove it entirely from your life. I love it when people become impassioned and enthusiastic about improving their health. There is no greater feeling for me than helping someone realize that they have the power to change their destiny by improving their health.

As someone who has lived through these changes myself, and helped others do the same, I sincerely hope that what I've provided in this book is exactly what you need to change the role of gluten in your life. Before we part ways, I want to remind you why it's important to stay focused on your goal of living gluten-free.

- Today, we're exposed to more gluten than ever before and it's changing how our bodies react to gluten.
- Gluten can be pure havoc on your digestive system but the overall effects on your health can be much more far-reaching.
- Everyone should work towards balancing their intake of gluten, even if they don't currently suffer any digestive-related issues from it.
- There are different degrees of gluten sensitivity, and each person is an individual.
- 60 days is all you need to turn all of this around.

I send you off now to begin this journey but know that any time you need reassurance, advice, or to reconnect with all the reasons for reducing or eliminating gluten from your life, this book is here to serve as your resource. You have all the tools you need to make the transformation. All that's left is to get started and do it.

I wish you nothing but success and great health. If you've enjoyed this book or find that it has been exactly what you've needed to finally take control over gluten, please consider leaving a review so that maybe this information will reach another person who needs it too.

FINAL WORDS

If you enjoyed this book and are eager to get into a complete and very thorough process also known as a detoxification process then we want to recommend that you consider grabbing Pureture's detoxification book if you haven't already. This book is where we will walk you through step by step to cleanse, detox, and reset each organ in a safe, thorough and proper order.

Go ahead and look for the title:

"6 Optimal Steps for Detoxification & Reset; Ultimate Plan to Cleanse & Heal all Body Organs for Lasting Results"

This book has included a program that will absolutely change your life and get you on track for a lifelong lifestyle of healthy habits and staying cleansed. It has been geared to heal the gut and to also implement positive habits that will live with you forever.

MESSAGE FROM PURETURE WITH PURETURE WELLNESS

Thank you for giving yourself an opportunity to experience a change in your life. If any questions arise, or if you simply have a comment, please feel free to contact me through the website at https://www.pureture.com/. At Pureture Wellness, my team's mission is to expand the healing process that has changed our own lives so that we may impact as many as we can. At the link provided below, you may find some of my other work and related literature on the website as well. You will also come across the coaching and training services I personally provide. I have worked with the human body for over a decade now and have been an athlete from a very young age. From nutritional coaching to fitness plan structures, or anything in between, please do not hesitate to contact us.

Cheers to optimal health and wellness!

~Pureture

Relevant Links

https://www.pureture.com

www.pureturewellness.com

REFERENCES

Addolorato G;Marsigli L;Capristo E;Caputo F;Dall'Aglio C;Baudanza P;. (1998, September/October). *Anxiety and depression: A common feature of health care seeking patients with irritable bowel syndrome and food allergy.* Retrieved November, from https://pubmed.ncbi.nlm.nih.gov/9840105/

Alaedini A;Okamoto H;Briani C;Wollenberg K;Shill HA;Bushara KO;Sander HW;Green PH;Hallett M;Latov N;. (2017, May). *Immune cross-reactivity in celiac disease: Antigliadin antibodies bind to neuronal synapsin I.* Retrieved from https://pubmed.ncbi.nlm.nih.gov/17475890/

Anxiety and Depression Association of America. (n.d.). Facts & *Statistics*. Retrieved November 30, 2020, from https://adaa.org/about-adaa/press-room/facts-statistics

Blumenthal, R. (2019, December 11). All Info - S.3021 - 116th Congress (2019-2020): *Gluten in Medicine Disclosure Act of 2019*. Retrieved from https://www.congress.gov/bill/116th-congress/senate-bill/3021/all-info?r=2

Capannolo A;Viscido A;Barkad MA;Valerii G;Ciccone F;Melideo D;Frieri G;Latella G;. (2015, May 30). *Non-Celiac Gluten Sensitivity among Patients Perceiving Gluten-Related Symptoms*. Retrieved from https://pubmed.ncbi.nlm.nih.gov/26043918/

Caproni, M., Bonciolini, V., D'Errico, A., Antiga, E., & Fabbri, P. (2012, May 30). *Celiac Disease and Dermatologic Manifestations: Many Skin Clue to Unfold Gluten-Sensitive Enteropathy*. Retrieved from https://www.hindawi.com/journals/grp/2012/952753/

Carabotti, M., Scirocco, A., Maselli, M., & Severi, C. (2015, April/May). *The gut-brain axis: Interactions between enteric microbiota, central and enteric nervous systems*. Retrieved from https://www.ncbi.nlm.nih.gov/pmc/articles/PMC4367209/

Catassi, C., Bai, J., Bonaz, B., Bouma, G., Calabrò, A., Carroccio, A., . . . Fasano, A. (2013, September 26). *Non-Celiac Gluten sensitivity: The new frontier of gluten related disorders*. Retrieved from https://www.ncbi.nlm.nih.gov/pmc/articles/PMC3820047/

Celiac Disease Foundation. (n.d.). *Non-Celiac Gluten/Wheat Sensitivity*. Retrieved from https://celiac.org/about-celiac-disease/related-conditions/non-celiac-wheat-gluten-sensitivity/

Celiac Disease Foundation. (n.d.). *Sources of Gluten*. Retrieved from https://celiac.org/gluten-free-living/what-is-gluten/sources-of-gluten/

Centers for Disease Control and Prevention. (2020, September 25). Data & *Statistics on Autism Spectrum Disorder*. Retrieved from https://www.cdc.gov/ncbddd/autism/data.html

Ch'ng CL;Jones MK;Kingham. (2007, October). *Celiac disease and autoimmune thyroid disease*. Retrieved from https://pubmed.ncbi.nlm.nih.gov/18056028/

Dimitrova AK;Ungaro RC;Lebwohl B;Lewis SK;Tennyson CA;Green MW;Babyatsky MW;Green PH;. (2012, November 5). *Prevalence of migraine in patients with celiac disease and inflammatory bowel disease*. Retrieved from https://pubmed.ncbi.nlm.nih.gov/23126519/

Dimitrova, A., Ungaro, R., Lebwohl, B., Lewis, S., Tennyson, C., Green, M., . . . Green, P. (2012, November 05). *Prevalence of Migraine in Patients With Celiac Disease and Inflammatory Bowel Disease*. Retrieved from https://headachejournal.onlinelibrary.wiley.com/doi/10.1111/j.1526-4610.2012.02260.x

Hadjivassiliou, M., Aeschlimann, P., Sanders, D., & Mäki, M. (2013, April). *Transglutaminase 6 antibodies in the diagnosis of gluten ataxia*: Request PDF. Retrieved from https://www.researchgate.net/publication/236193177_Transglutaminase_6_antibodies_in_the_diagnosis_of_gluten_ataxia

Jackson, J., Eaton, W., Cascella, N., Fasano, A., & Kelly, D. (2012, March). *Neurologic and psychiatric manifestations of celiac disease and gluten sensitivity.* Retrieved from https://www.ncbi.nlm.nih.gov/pmc/articles/PMC3641836/

Jackson, J., Eaton, W., Cascella, N., Fasano, A., & Kelly, D. (2012, March). *Neurologic and psychiatric manifestations of celiac disease and gluten sensitivity.* Retrieved from https://www.ncbi.nlm.nih.gov/pmc/articles/PMC3641836/

Makharia, A., Catassi, C., & Makharia, G. (2015, December 10). *The Overlap between Irritable Bowel Syndrome and Non-Celiac Gluten Sensitivity: A Clinical Dilemma.* Retrieved from https://www.ncbi.nlm.nih.gov/pmc/articles/PMC4690093/

Mikkelsen K;Stojanovska L;Apostolopoulos V. (n.d.). *The Effects of Vitamin B in Depression.* Retrieved from https://pubmed.ncbi.nlm.nih.gov/27655070/

Mu, Q., Kirby, J., Reilly, C., & Luo, X. (2017, May 23). *Leaky Gut As a Danger Signal for Autoimmune Diseases.*

Retrieved from https://www.ncbi.nlm.nih.gov/pmc/articles/PMC5440529/

Muneer, A. (2016, January). *Bipolar Disorder: Role of Inflammation and the Development of Disease Biomarkers.* Retrieved from https://www.ncbi.nlm.nih.gov/pmc/articles/PMC4701682/

National Institute of Mental Health. (n.d.). *Bipolar Disorder.* Retrieved from https://www.nimh.nih.gov/health/topics/bipolar-disorder/index.shtml

Niederhofer, H. (2011, June 16). *Association of Attention-Deficit/Hyperactivity Disorder and Celiac Disease: A Brief Report.* Retrieved from https://www.psychiatrist.com/PCC/article/Pages/association-attention-deficit-hyperactivity-disorder.aspx

Office On Women's Health. (2019, April 01). *Autoimmune diseases.* Retrieved from https://www.womenshealth.gov/a-z-topics/autoimmune-diseases

Osborne, P. (2020, June 19). *Gluten Sensitivity and Vertigo/Meniere's Disease.* Retrieved from https://www.glutenfreesociety.org/gluten-sensitivity-and-vertigomenieres-disease/

Porcelli, B., Verdino, V., Bossini, L., Terzuoli, L., & Fagiolini, A. (2014, October 16). *Celiac and non-celiac gluten sensitivity: A review on the association with schizophrenia and mood disorders.* Retrieved from https://www.ncbi.nlm. nih.gov/pmc/articles/PMC4389040/

Rezania, K., MD. (2010, Spring). *Celiac Neuropathy.* Retrieved from https://www.cureceliacdisease.org/wp-content/uploads/0410CeliacCtr_News.pdf

Riffkin, R. (2020, January 06). *One in Five Americans Include Gluten-Free Foods in Diet.* Retrieved from https://news.gallup.com/poll/184307/one-five-americans-include-gluten-free-foods-diet.aspx?utm_source=Well-Being

Rojas, M., Restrepo-Jiménez, P., Monsalve, D., Pacheco, Y., Acosta-Ampudia, Y., Ramírez-Santana, C., . . . Anaya, J. (2018, October 26). *Molecular mimicry and autoimmunity.* Retrieved from https://www.sciencedirect.com/science/article/pii/S0896841118305365

T;, R. (1998, October). Dermatitis herpetiformis: *Coeliac disease of the skin.* Retrieved from https://pubmed.ncbi.nlm.nih.gov/9814827/

Volta U;Bardella MT;Calabrò A;Troncone R;Corazza GR; ;. (n.d.). *An Italian prospective multicenter survey on patients suspected of having non-celiac gluten sensitivity.* Retrieved from https://pubmed.ncbi.nlm.nih.gov/24885375/

World Health Organization. (2014, February 11). *Headache disorders: How common are headaches?* Retrieved from https://www.who.int/news-room/q-a-detail/headache-disorders-how-common-are-headaches

Zis, P., Julian, T., & Hadjivassiliou, M. (2018, October 06). *Headache Associated with Coeliac Disease: A Systematic Review and Meta-Analysis.* Retrieved from https://www.mdpi.com/2072-6643/10/10/1445

Zis, P., Rao, D., Sarrigiannis, P., Aeschlimann, P., Aeschlimann, D., Sanders, D., . . . Hadjivassiliou, M. (2017, August 10). *Transglutaminase 6 antibodies in gluten neuropathy.* Retrieved from https://www.sciencedirect.com/science/article/abs/pii/S1590865817310095

Printed in Great Britain
by Amazon